PRESENTED TO:

_____

FROM:

_____

DATE:

_____

DEVOTIONS *for*

YOUNG READERS

CARA WHITNEY

THOMAS NELSON
Since 1798

Tommy Nelson, PO Box 141000, Nashville, TN 37214

Published in Nashville, Tennessee, by Tommy Nelson. Tommy Nelson is an imprint of Thomas Nelson. Thomas Nelson is a registered trademark of HarperCollins Christian Publishing, Inc.

Published in association with the literary agency of WordServe Literary Group, Ltd., www.wordserveliterary.com.

Adapted from *Unbridled Faith: 100 Devotions from the Horse Farm* by Cara Whitney.

Photos on pages 9, 11, 13, 15, 21, 23, 27, 29, 31, 35, 39, 41, 43, 45, 47, 51, 53, 55, 57, 59, 61, 63, 65, 69, 71, 73, 75, 79, 81, 83, 85, 87, 89, 93, 95, 99, 101, 103, 105, 107, 109, 113, 117, 119, 121, 123, 129, 131, 133, 135, 137, 141, 143, 145, 147, 149, 153, 155, 163, 165, 171, 175, and 185 are by Erik Johnson, www.erikjohnsonphotography.com.

Remaining interior images and cover photo used under license from Shutterstock.

Tommy Nelson titles may be purchased in bulk for educational, business, fund-raising, or sales promotional use. For information, please e-mail SpecialMarkets@ThomasNelson.com.

Scripture quotations marked CEV are from the Contemporary English Version. Copyright © 1991, 1992, 1995 by American Bible Society. Used by permission.

Scripture quotations marked ICB are from the International Children's Bible®. Copyright © 1986, 1988, 1999, 2015 by Thomas Nelson. Used by permission. All rights reserved.

Scripture quotations marked NCV are from the New Century Version®. © 2005 by Thomas Nelson. Used by permission. All rights reserved.

Scripture quotations marked NIV are from the Holy Bible, New International Version®, NIV®. Copyright © 1973, 1978, 1984, 2011 by Biblica, Inc.® Used by permission of Zondervan. All rights reserved worldwide. www.Zondervan.com. The "NIV" and "New International Version" are trademarks registered in the United States Patent and Trademark Office by Biblica, Inc.®

Scripture quotations marked NLT are from the Holy Bible, New Living Translation. © 1996, 2004, 2007, 2013, 2015 by Tyndale House Foundation. Used by permission of Tyndale House Publishers, Inc., Carol Stream, Illinois 60188. All rights reserved.

ISBN: 978-1-4002-1781-6
ISBN: 978-1-4002-1778-6 (e-Book)

Library of Congress Cataloging-in-Publication Data on file

Printed in India

23 24   REP   10 9 8 7 6 5 4 3 2

Mfr: REP / Haryana, India / June 2023 / PO #12209562

*To my Aunt Julie, who shined her little
light into so many dark rooms.*

*Arnie, Char, and Orlando, for
encouraging me to saddle up.*

*Shirley, for being my role
model for gentleness.*

Beamon, for being my spiritual driver.

*And to my Little Beedy, for loving us
so well because you love God first.*

WELCOME TO THE BARN PARTY

My funny horse is the life of the barn party. His name is Sven, and he loves to "talk." If he sees me, Sven will whinny. And even though he's a pretty big guy, his whinny is very wimpy. One of the funny things about Sven is what he does when he wants something on the other side of the wire fence. He lies on the fence until it collapses and then rolls over the top of it. Sven's funny ways give joy to everyone at the barn.

If you're like me, you find joy in a lot of different ways—through your animals, family, and friends. However, if you and I want to share the joy of being in heaven, we need to find our greatest joy in salvation. Jesus told us there will be "more joy in heaven over one sinner who changes his heart and life, than over ninety-nine good people who don't need to change" (Luke 15:7 NCV).

Our upside-down culture prizes wearing trendy clothes, having the latest smartphone, being rich and famous, and belonging to the in-crowd. But as citizens of God's kingdom, we should put our salvation—and the salvation of those around us—at the top of our lists of things that bring us joy. Think of it: the angels have a party in heaven when just one of us chooses to follow Jesus. And you can bet that when you accept Jesus as your Savior, those angels will throw a party to celebrate you too! Now, doesn't that make you want to kick up your heels?

LORD, THANK YOU FOR THE GIFT OF SALVATION. I
WANT TO BE PART OF THOSE GREAT CELEBRATIONS
IN HEAVEN WITH YOU, AMEN.

IT'S OKAY TO NOT BE OKAY

"I NO LONGER CALL YOU SERVANTS, BECAUSE A SERVANT DOES NOT KNOW HIS MASTER'S BUSINESS. INSTEAD, I HAVE CALLED YOU FRIENDS."
JOHN 15:15 NIV

Horses are amazing animals. When I feel sad or upset, my horses seem to sense my pain. They turn their ears toward me and even lean into me. In those moments, they aren't just sweet creatures to ride, train, and enjoy. They are my friends.

Still, sometimes our hurt feelings and sadness are just too big. Even the comfort of our horses can't ease the pain. Maybe you're upset because your mom or dad lost a job or someone you care about is sick. Or maybe you had an argument with your best friend. Whatever it is, some troubles need more help than horse hugs.

With God, we don't have to pretend everything is okay. He longs to be the "friend who sticks closer than a brother" (Proverbs 18:24 NIV). He created us, so He knows us better than we know ourselves. We can be honest and real with Him. And His power can help us get through tough times. We just have to be humble enough to admit we need Him.

You are not big enough to fix every problem on your own. Run into the arms of your heavenly Father, who loves you. Trust Him to be the most faithful, best Friend you've ever had.

Lord, thank You for being not only my Creator and Savior but also my best Friend, amen.

LISTEN AND PRAY

THEN THEY SAT ON THE GROUND WITH HIM FOR SEVEN
DAYS AND SEVEN NIGHTS. NO ONE SAID A WORD TO HIM,
BECAUSE THEY SAW HOW GREAT HIS SUFFERING WAS.
JOB 2:13 NIV

When I brush my horse, I am actually telling him my problems. My hands and my heart tell him what I'm feeling. In return, my horse leans into me. He seems to say, "It's going to be okay." With just his presence, he comforts me. He doesn't have to say a word.

Not long ago, scientists did an amazing study. It showed that horses can tell when we're happy or sad. They see our faces and know whether we want to play or need comfort.[1] If only we humans were as good at knowing what our friends need!

In the Old Testament, Job was blessed with wealth, friends, and family. Then Satan began to test him. Satan took away everything Job had—his money, his family, even his health. Job's wife told him to curse God and die. Then his friends came around. They comforted Job just by being there and listening.

But then Job's friends began to speak. They suggested that Job must have done something bad to deserve all his suffering. They told him what they thought was wrong and what he should do about it. The more they said, the more upset Job became.

Too many times, we are like Job's so-called friends. We are uncomfortable with silence, so we rush to fill the quiet with our own opinions. What if we prayed for God's wisdom before we spoke? It just might make all the difference.

If we wish to be godly encouragers, we must not speak until we have truly listened and prayed. Our words do have a place when we are trying to help someone. But we should let our prayers do the talking when we are not sure what to say.

LORD, USE ME TO ENCOURAGE AND COMFORT
OTHERS—ESPECIALLY THOSE WHO ARE HURTING.
REMIND ME TO PRAY BEFORE I SPEAK. ABOVE ALL,
SHOW ME HOW TO SIMPLY LISTEN, AMEN.

BUCKED OFF OUR HIGH HORSE

HUMBLE YOURSELVES BEFORE THE LORD,
AND HE WILL LIFT YOU UP.
JAMES 4:10 NIV

I thought I knew what my horse Nelson was thinking. Even though I showered him with care and love, the truth is Nelson couldn't have cared less about me. While my friend held the lunge line—a long rope tied to the horse to help control him—Nelson bucked me off! I went on a wild ride, sailing through the air and landing in the sand. My friend, who was still holding the lunge line, was dragged across the arena. I was unhurt, but my ego took a beating that day.

Sometimes we start to think we have it all figured out. That's called "getting up on our high horse." And *that's* when we need to be bucked off. We should never forget how great God is and how much He forgives us. Jesus' perfect life, kindness, and death on the cross should remind us that God is the *only* One who has it all figured out.

Being humble is hard. Pride sneaks in when we start to think we are strong and can handle things better than God. As believers, we must walk in the footsteps of Jesus and place ourselves under His loving guidance. The Bible has some harsh words about pride: "It is wise to hate pride and bragging, evil ways and lies" (Proverbs 8:13 ICB).

Pride is also a sin that leads to other sins. When we're filled with pride, we think we're better than others and then we start acting like it. We should surrender to God daily, asking for forgiveness from our pride. He will help us deal with life and love the people around us selflessly. As we walk in humility, we can enjoy living the way God created us to live.

What are you waiting for? Climb off your high horse, and fall on your knees before Jesus.

LORD, FORGIVE ME FOR SOMETIMES THINKING I'M BETTER THAN OTHERS OR THAT I DON'T NEED YOU. TEACH ME TO BE HUMBLE AS I OBEY YOU DAILY, AMEN.

THE ONE-TRICK PONY

I AM SURE THAT NOTHING CAN SEPARATE US FROM GOD'S
LOVE—NOT LIFE OR DEATH, NOT ANGELS OR SPIRITS, NOT
THE PRESENT OR THE FUTURE, AND NOT POWERS ABOVE OR
POWERS BELOW. NOTHING IN ALL CREATION CAN SEPARATE
US FROM GOD'S LOVE FOR US IN CHRIST JESUS OUR LORD!
ROMANS 8:38-39 CEV

Horse training is about understanding the horse, not about tricks, food, or force. A good trainer gets to know the animal. The trainer gently works with the horse, forming trust day by day. Bad trainers, however, use fear to force a horse to do what they want. They believe being in total control is the goal.

In much the same way, Satan is like a bad trainer. He uses fear and lies to try to force us to do what he wants. And what he wants is to distract us from following God. But Satan is a one-trick pony: using fear and lies is the only thing he knows how to do. Like a bad trainer, Satan offers false, right-now rewards that can't compare to God's eternal promises. Don't give in. During those moments, remember the cross. Hold tight to the truths found in Scripture.

Nothing can separate us from God's love. When we confess our sins and trust Jesus as Lord and Savior, we can be sure that we will spend forever with Him: "God saved you by his grace when you believed. And you can't take credit for this; it is a gift from God. Salvation is not a reward for the good things we have done, so none of us can boast about it" (Ephesians 2:8–9 NLT).

Jesus gave His life so we could be forgiven of our sins and spend forever with Him. But that's not all He did. Jesus also gives us the power to run away from the devil and his tricks. With Jesus, we can have a rich and joyful life here on earth.

LORD, STEER ME CLEAR OF THE DEVIL'S TRICKS. THANK YOU FOR GENTLY TEACHING ME THE WAY I SHOULD LIVE, AMEN.

SKITTISH

WHEN JESUS AND HIS DISCIPLES HAD FINISHED
EATING, HE ASKED, "SIMON SON OF JOHN,
DO YOU LOVE ME MORE THAN THE OTHERS DO?"
SIMON PETER ANSWERED, "YES, LORD, YOU KNOW I DO!"
"THEN FEED MY LAMBS," JESUS SAID.
JOHN 21:15 CEV

Sometimes I think my horse fears two things: objects that move and objects that don't. If you look up *skittish* in the dictionary, you'll see that it means "easily frightened." Plus you'll probably see my horse's picture next to the definition!

And on certain days, I'm skittish too. I trip myself up with doubts and worries. *Did I do that right? What will my friends think?* I run away at the slightest things. Do you ever have days like that? Fear is a real and powerful force in our lives, and Satan uses it to trip us up. The devil's goal isn't always to hurt us directly but rather to get us to believe that God is not trustworthy.

Peter was one of Satan's victims.

Peter was so afraid after Jesus was arrested that he said he didn't even know Him—three different times! After the resurrection, Jesus met Peter again and asked Peter if he loved Him—three times. And three times Peter said that he did.

After our Lord had risen from the dead, He stood eye to eye with Peter. Jesus gave His disciple a second chance. Once Peter confessed his love, Jesus gave him the job of looking out for others (His lambs).

It would not always be an easy job, but as long as Peter didn't give in to his fear and trusted in God each day, he would succeed.

While the devil's tricks never change, neither do God's promises. Peter was frozen with fear, but later he was restored to faith. And as we learn from the book of Acts, God used Peter to bring thousands of people to Jesus. Satan lost that battle.

Is fear pulling you down? Tell your fears to Jesus, and trust Him to keep you safe.

LORD, FORGIVE ME FOR THE TIMES I HAVE DOUBTED YOU.
HELP ME BE FEARLESS IN FOLLOWING YOU, AMEN.

STAY SALTY

> *"YOU ARE THE SALT OF THE EARTH."*
> MATTHEW 5:13 NIV

Did you know that horses, like people, need extra salt when the weather is hot? And even when it's not hot outside, my horse *loves* salt.

In Jesus' day, salt was a form of money. It was expensive and hard to get. Jesus understood the value of salt. He called His believers the "salt of the earth" because we're so valuable to Him. For us Christians to lose our saltiness means that the good news of Jesus isn't adding flavor to our lives. Instead, the world is adding its flavor to us. Maybe it's because we quit spending time with God each day and play on our devices instead. Or maybe we focus on everything we don't have instead of the gifts God has freely given us. Whatever the reason, people who lose their saltiness—who do not protect God's truth in their lives from the ideas of this world—will have little flavor left to bless the lives around them.

The truth is, people who don't know what the Bible says easily fall for whatever lies the world tells them. If they don't make it a habit to read the Bible, these people can quickly lose their saltiness. They can't stand strong in the faith, and they can't be confident in telling others about Christ. Life will offer all kinds of flavors—good, not-so-good, and just plain terrible—but *it's your salty side that God loves most*. Get into God's Word—and get salty!

Lord, I don't ever want to lose Your flavor in my life. Help me grow in faith and wisdom, and let my light shine before others so that they may see Your salty goodness, amen.

Salty. Yum!

WATER CROSSINGS

"When you pass through the waters, I will be with you; and when you pass through the rivers, they will not sweep over you."
Isaiah 43:2 NIV

Water crossings are not my horse Sven's favorite thing to do. He plants his feet and won't go in. Sven will tiptoe up to the water and back, then step left and right. He'll do anything *but* put his foot in. I have been told horses can't tell how deep water is unless they go in. In that case, maybe I need to be working on getting Sven to trust me more. Sven needs to believe that I won't ask him to cross where it's not safe to go.

Throughout our lives, you and I will face plenty of situations where we're not sure it's safe. Some obstacles will be tougher than others, and some will seem downright impossible to get through.

God will not put an obstacle or situation in front of you that He can't handle. And God promises to be with you over, around, and through all of your challenges. As Psalm 23:4 says, "Even though I walk through the darkest valley, I will fear no evil, for you are with me; your rod and your staff, they comfort me" (NIV).

If you struggle to trust God, take the first step by diving into His Word today. The real joy in life and in faith comes when we are willing to step forward and get our feet wet. Then, when troubles do come, take your cries and prayers to Jesus. His mighty power will keep your head above the troubled waters of this world.

Lord, give me the strength to handle the obstacles in my life. I will trust that You are with me—just as Your Word promises, amen.

ONE OF A KIND

GOD HAS ALSO GIVEN EACH OF US DIFFERENT GIFTS TO USE.
ROMANS 12:6 CEV

We all have our opinions on what horse breed is best. God designed each breed differently, from little Shetlands to huge Clydesdales. All of them are wonderful, but none have the same personalities, talents, or abilities. For instance, Fjords (say *fee-ORDs*) and Shetlands have a pony personality. Ponies are kind of like puppies—they can be naughty, for sure, but when they see you've reached your limits, they switch gears into charming mode. Even though ponies might have big personalities, they are tiny. You would never ask or expect a Shetland pony to pull a heavy wagon.

Like the many differences between horse breeds, there are all kinds of God-given gifts in the body of Christ (the church). The Creator gives each of us a unique personality and talents in order to serve Him. No one's gift is better than yours, and yours isn't better than anyone else's. After all, you are a one-of-a-kind masterpiece, the very workmanship of God (Ephesians 2:10), knit together in your mother's womb, fearfully and wonderfully made (Psalm 139:13–14).

Whether you sing, teach younger kids, draw, cook, clean, or encourage, you are unique. You have been made by a loving God, and He has given you specific abilities. He also gave you the gift of eternal life through Jesus. And He gave you opportunities to tell the world the good news about Him. Don't waste a moment! Get out there and use your God-given talents today.

Lord, I praise You and thank You for giving me one-of-a-kind talents and gifts. Help me use them for You and use them well, amen.

STAND STRONG

YOU ARE TEMPTED IN THE SAME WAY THAT EVERYONE ELSE IS TEMPTED. BUT GOD CAN BE TRUSTED NOT TO LET YOU BE TEMPTED TOO MUCH, AND HE WILL SHOW YOU HOW TO ESCAPE FROM YOUR TEMPTATIONS.
1 CORINTHIANS 10:13 CEV

During trail rides, my horse Sven has perfected a trick I call the "sneak and eat." When he thinks no one is looking, Sven grabs the first green thing he sees and tries to eat it. No matter how big or small the snack, the temptation is just too much. The next thing you know, he'll have an entire branch sticking out of his mouth.

We all know about temptation. The first man and woman, Adam and Eve, fell into sin after they were tempted, even though they lived in a picture-perfect world. And Jesus was tempted, although He did not sin.

Thankfully, God does not allow His children to be tempted beyond what we can handle with His help. The fact is, we *will* wrestle with sin in this life. And we won't ever completely defeat it until we meet the Lord in heaven. However, **because Jesus died on the cross, sin doesn't have to be the boss of our lives** (Romans 6:13–14).

The next time you feel tempted, ask God for strength to say no. What's more, ask Him what to do *before* you get tempted. Maybe you need to choose different friends, find a new way to spend your free time, or just get more sleep. When God gives you answers, be sure to follow through on cutting out those things that tempt you to sin.

The devil is powerful, but God is greater. He doesn't promise that the choice to say no will be easy. But if you ask for His help, He will give you the strength to stand strong—and the devil will run away.

LORD, PROTECT ME FROM THE DEVIL. PLEASE GIVE ME THE POWER TO SAY NO TO TEMPTATION AND SIN. I WANT TO KNOW, LOVE, SERVE, AND FOLLOW YOU, AMEN.

SET FREE

HAPPY IS THE PERSON WHOSE SINS ARE FORGIVEN,
WHOSE WRONGS ARE PARDONED. HAPPY IS THE PERSON
WHOM THE LORD DOES NOT CONSIDER GUILTY. IN
THAT PERSON THERE IS NOTHING FALSE.
PSALM 32:1–2 ICB

It doesn't matter how much we want to continue riding, trying to push an exhausted horse farther is not going to get us anywhere. I've learned the hard way that it's always best to end the ride on a high note. If my horse's patience is growing shorter, I need to stop for the day. Otherwise, I'll waste my energy, and my horse's, trying to get somewhere else.

In much the same way, do you find yourself asking God over and over to forgive you for something He has already forgiven? If you have accepted Jesus as your Savior and repented, that sin is forgiven. Period.

Maybe what we really need is to learn how to forgive *ourselves*. When we sin, one prayer asking for forgiveness may seem too easy. But it's not. It's the devil who causes us to think more about our sin than our Savior.

We have to choose whether we are going to believe God or the devil. If we trade self-confidence for God-confidence, it will change our lives. "Let us then approach God's throne of grace with confidence, so that we may receive mercy and find grace to help us in our time of need" (Hebrews 4:16 NIV).

Jesus already paid for our sins when He died on a cross. Colossians 2:13–14 says, "God forgave all our sins. We owed a debt because we broke God's laws. That debt listed all the rules we failed to follow. But God forgave us that debt. He took away that debt and nailed it to the cross" (ICB).

Until you let go of your past sins and trust God's love and forgiveness, you will never leave the stall. No sin is too big for Almighty God to forgive. Trust in Him. He has already set you free.

LORD, I PRAISE YOU THAT MY SIN IS FORGIVEN. I DON'T HAVE TO KEEP WORRYING ABOUT THE PAST. HELP ME TRUST YOUR LOVE AND FORGIVENESS, AMEN.

TOO MANY TREATS

TRUST THE LORD WITH ALL YOUR HEART.
PROVERBS 3:5 NCV

It's tough to say no to my pony Tucker when he wants a treat.

I bet you're familiar with the look ponies give their owner when they want something: sad eyes, followed by all that nickering for our attention. I used to give in to this—every time. But I ended up giving Tucker so many treats that I made him sick. After that, I became wiser about what I gave him, and he was healthier for it.

Like Tucker, we don't always know what will truly make us happy. If God granted our every wish, more than likely He would end up doing us more harm than good.

Fortunately for us, God is a Father we can trust to know what's really good for us *and* what is bad for us. God knows whether an invitation to *that* party, a spot on *that* team, or a friendship with *that* person will help us or hurt us in the end. Just remember, if He does say no, it's because He has something even better planned. We can trust Him to know exactly what we need when we need it—and to give it to us.

If God has said no to you, thank Him today for protecting you from *that* thing you were so sure you had to have. Then praise Him for blessing you with the good thing He knew you needed.

LORD, THANK YOU FOR KNOWING WHAT'S
BEST AND GIVING ME WHAT I NEED—NOT
ALWAYS WHAT I WANT. HELP ME TRUST YOU
FROM THE BOTTOM OF MY HEART, AMEN.

A LESSON FROM A HORSE

> "SO BE CAREFUL! IF ANOTHER FOLLOWER SINS, WARN HIM,
> AND IF HE IS SORRY AND STOPS SINNING, FORGIVE HIM.
> IF HE SINS AGAINST YOU SEVEN TIMES IN ONE DAY AND
> SAYS THAT HE IS SORRY EACH TIME, FORGIVE HIM."
> LUKE 17:3–4 NCV

Ramming our feet into the stirrups. Pulling on our horses' mouths with the reins. Losing our tempers. It's nice to know that horses forgive us. A few times, I have accused a horse of being naughty, only to discover later that he was actually reacting to something painful. I have lost my temper and fussed at horses. I accidentally hit one with a rope. Another time I hit one in the face with a gate while opening it. Thank goodness they were not injured, but I still felt terrible.

The truth is, horses will carry us, but they refuse to carry the weight of a grudge against their frustrating humans. Even horses' friendships with each other are not hurt when they are pushed around by another horse. It's the way they're built.

Forgiveness is so easy for horses, yet so difficult for us humans. The truth is, people make mistakes not only with horses but also with each other. While forgiving someone can be difficult, holding a grudge is worse. Carrying around hard feelings makes us bitter and unhappy. I've heard someone say that holding on to bitterness and unforgiveness is like eating rat poison—and then waiting for the rat to die!

Forgiveness is not only about giving grace to others; it's also about our own spiritual growth. Because God has forgiven all our sins, we should not refuse to forgive others: "Do not be angry with each other, but forgive each other. If someone does wrong to you, then forgive him. Forgive each other because the Lord forgave you" (Colossians 3:13 ICB).

If you have been carrying around the burden of a grudge, it's time to ask God to help you set things right. Take a lesson from your horse, and learn to forgive.

LORD, I PRAISE
YOU FOR
FORGIVING
ME. HELP ME
DO THE SAME
AND FORGIVE
OTHERS, AMEN.

TRUST THE DRIVER

WHO KNOWS IF PERHAPS YOU WERE MADE
QUEEN FOR JUST SUCH A TIME AS THIS?
ESTHER 4:14 NLT

As a general rule, horses don't like trailers. Some of them don't want to go in, and some don't like coming out. I have horses that plant their feet at the trailer door and refuse to move. The trick is to walk them away and take another run at it. Sometimes you need to load their buddy first or bribe them with food.

Why are most horses not fond of trailers? Because they aren't sure where they are going or what is waiting for them when they get there. The ride doesn't make sense to the horse. The driver knows where the horse is going, but the horse doesn't.

Much like our horse friends, we can sometimes feel as if we're being pushed, pulled, and taken for a ride we don't want to be on. But consider this: God has placed us where we are right now for a reason. The part He has given us to play and the challenges we face don't always make sense. Sometimes we feel like giving up. Don't do it! Take heart and keep going. Who knows? Like Queen Esther in today's verse, you may have been planted in your class, school, church, family, or neighborhood "for just such a time as this." Esther was able to save her people, the Jews, from being killed because she had been chosen to be the wife of the king at an important time.

God wants to use you for His glory too. As a Christian, your life is not your own. It belongs to the One who created you, and He has a plan just for you. Trust the Driver, because He knows where you're going.

LORD, GIVE ME THE STRENGTH TO TRUST YOU MORE— EVEN WHEN LIFE DOESN'T MAKE SENSE. GIVE ME THE RIGHT ATTITUDE, AND HELP ME KNOW THAT I AM RIGHT WHERE YOU WANT ME, AMEN.

BLACK BEAUTY

God used the Good News that we preached to call
you to be saved. He called you so that you can
share in the glory of our Lord Jesus Christ.
2 Thessalonians 2:14 icb

My favorite horses are the old ones. Giving them a nice place to live out their years has been very good for my heart. Horses like feeling safe, and I like taking care of them. They keep my heart soft. In the past, I didn't let myself care about others too much. I thought that a hard heart would keep me safe from pain and disappointment. But although a soft heart does feel more pain, it also feels more joy.

My love for older horses most likely began when I first read the story *Black Beauty*. Throughout this wonderful tale, a character named Joe longs to find a horse, Black Beauty, from his past. At one point, Joe walks right past Beauty at a horse sale and doesn't notice him! But by the end of the adventure, Beauty finds his "savior." He lives the rest of his life with Joe.

There are many times in our lives when God reaches out to us, but we miss our opportunities to connect with Him. We may decide we've messed up too many times. Or we may believe deep down that we are not worth saving. But understand this: God will never stop loving you. He will never stop wanting you close to Him. Nothing you have ever done or will ever do is going to change that. Study the stories about Jesus and His journey to the cross. He suffered every bit of that—the beatings, the shame, the terrible death—for me and for *you*.

Do you want to live the rest of your life with Someone who will always be with you and who will never sell you out? Say yes to God, and get to know your Savior today.

LORD, I'M SO GLAD YOU WANT ME TO BE YOUR CHILD.
I WANT TO KNOW YOU AND LIVE WITH YOU FOREVER.
THANK YOU FOR THE HOME I HAVE IN YOU, AMEN.

ONE-EYED ROANIE

SEE HOW VERY MUCH OUR FATHER LOVES US, FOR HE
CALLS US HIS CHILDREN, AND THAT IS WHAT WE ARE!
1 JOHN 3:1 NLT

My best friend from childhood was a one-eyed quarter horse named Roanie. She was loyal and sweet. Roanie came to me when I was twelve years old and desperately needed a friend. When we went on rides together, she took care of me. One time we got in a nest of bees, and she did not buck because I was on her back. She just took the pain of all those stings.

At first glance, the world would see my "broken" horse as having little value. But if you were to ask me, her kind heart and gentle spirit made her *priceless*. And that's how God looks at us too.

He sees us the way He has always seen us: as His precious children. Parents love their children more than kids will ever understand (at least, until you have kids of your own). What's more, parents love their children no matter how they act or what they do—good, bad, or ugly. Think about this: ***God loves us even more than a parent loves a child.*** It's mind-blowing when you think about it.

Have you ever doubted your own worth? If so, remember how much God values you. He sent His only Son to live on this earth, to die, and to be raised to life again—all to save you. God the Father paid the ultimate price to rescue us from our sin.

Don't let anyone tell you what you are worth. God has loved you since He knit you together in your mother's womb (Psalm 139:13). And He will love you for all eternity.

When the world makes you feel like a broken, one-eyed horse, remember this: you are priceless to God.

LORD, THANK YOU FOR LOVING ME JUST AS I AM.
THANK YOU FOR DECLARING THAT I AM A CHILD OF
GOD AND THAT I AM PRICELESS IN YOUR EYES, AMEN.

FOLLOW THE TRAIL MAP

Everything in the Scriptures is God's Word. All of it is useful for teaching and helping people and for correcting them and showing them how to live. The Scriptures train God's servants to do all kinds of good deeds.
2 Timothy 3:16–17 CEV

Your saddle creaks softly beneath you as your horse moves at a steady pace. With each step, your body loosens a little, rocking with the rhythm of the trail ride—and you can't help but feel at peace with the world. It's just you and your horse in the wilderness. The sunshine melts away your stress, and the fresh, pine-scented air perks up your senses. *Perfect.*

But suddenly you panic. *The map!* you think. *I forgot the trail map! What if we get lost? How will we find our way home? This is bad!*

As we travel through life, it's easy to get so busy that we forget to prepare for the journey ahead. We get caught up in the details of everyday living—school, homework, and tests, practices, church, and chores. We forget the One who is able to make us wise, strong, and godly. We go our own way, and we forget to talk to the One who knows what's around the bend and the exact route we should take.

God has given us the perfect trail map to get us safely through life: the Bible. Dotting the pages of Scripture (like trail markers along the way) are God's promises. They encourage us to keep going and warn us away from danger. God knows the way because He *is* the Way (John 14:6).

Start reading the Bible today. When you follow the Lord's trail map, He will deliver you safely home to heaven. And consider this: not only did God give us the map, He created the trails!

LORD, SOMETIMES I SET OFF ON THE JOURNEY WTTHOUT SEEKING YOUR GUIDANCE FIRST. HELP ME MAKE READING THE BIBLE A PART OF EVERY DAY. SPEAK TO ME THROUGH YOUR WORD SO THAT I MAY BE READY TO DO EVERY GOOD WORK, AMEN.

JUST AS YOU ARE

LORD, YOU WILL HAVE MERCY ON US AGAIN.
YOU WILL CONQUER OUR SINS. YOU WILL THROW
AWAY ALL OUR SINS INTO THE DEEPEST SEA.
MICAH 7:19 ICB

One of my favorite things about horses and donkeys is that they couldn't care less about what you've done or where you've been. When one of my four-legged friends sees me, he neighs and calls out to tell me he loves me, no matter what. Isn't that what we love about our dogs too? They are always *so* glad to see us. Animals love us without us having to do a thing. They accept us just as we are.

As much as our horses love us, **that love is nothing compared to the love Jesus has for us.** He loves us no matter what. He doesn't hold the past against us. He doesn't wave our sins in front of us to make us feel guilty so we'll act right. Now, the devil will do his best to hold the past over our heads and keep us feeling terrible. But as we come humbly before God, asking for forgiveness, He will throw our sins into the sea. God will take away our fears and our feelings of guilt. "How great is God's love for all who worship him? Greater than the distance between heaven and earth! How far has the LORD taken our sins from us? Farther than the distance from east to west!" (Psalm 103:11–12 CEV).

We don't have to be perfect for God. He loves us just as we are. The best part is, He gives us a way out of our sins. Through Christ, we can be completely forgiven.

So accept the never-ending love of the Father. He is waiting for you with open arms!

LORD, THANK YOU FOR YOUR MERCY AND GRACE.
THANK YOU FOR FORGIVING MY SIN AND FOR
LOVING ME NO MATTER WHAT, AMEN.

THE EXTRAORDINARY ORDINARY

ONE DAY AS JESUS WAS WALKING ALONG THE SHORE OF
THE SEA OF GALILEE, HE SAW TWO BROTHERS—SIMON,
ALSO CALLED PETER, AND ANDREW—THROWING A NET
INTO THE WATER, FOR THEY FISHED FOR A LIVING.
JESUS CALLED OUT TO THEM, "COME, FOLLOW ME, AND
I WILL SHOW YOU HOW TO FISH FOR PEOPLE!"
MATTHEW 4:18–19 NLT

My horse has mended a broken heart a time or two. It's sad that some people would say I own an "ordinary horse." He's never accomplished anything that would make him a champion in the eyes of the world. But to me, he is a champion healer.

God has a habit of taking what the world sees as ordinary and using it to perform His greatest miracles. Ordinary horses don't know they're ordinary, so why would we ever think *we* are just ordinary? The Bible makes it clear that we are extraordinary. And *God designed each one of us to do extraordinary things for His kingdom.*

When Jesus called Peter and Andrew to come and follow Him, they were just "ordinary" fishermen. But He had a plan for them. I'm sure they never expected to be world-changers. Maybe they followed Jesus because they believed He was a prophet or because He was just great to be around. Perhaps they were simply sick of fishing. Who knows what was going through their minds?

However, in a few short years, God would use these two—and others—to spread the gospel of Christ to thousands of people. Peter even became one of the leaders Jesus used to build the New Testament church.

God transformed the lives of those "ordinary" fishermen and turned them into powerful missionaries. Just imagine what He can do with *you*. Go out into the world with excitement, in His power, and get ready to be extraordinary today.

LORD, THANK YOU FOR MAKING ME ANYTHING BUT ORDINARY. I WANT TO BE A FISHER OF PEOPLE JUST LIKE PETER AND ANDREW. HELP ME GO OUT AND DO EXTRAORDINARY THINGS FOR YOU, AMEN.

FOREVER CONTENTMENT

I HAVE LEARNED THE SECRET OF BEING CONTENT IN ANY
AND EVERY SITUATION, WHETHER WELL FED OR HUNGRY,
WHETHER LIVING IN PLENTY OR IN WANT. I CAN DO
ALL THIS THROUGH HIM WHO GIVES ME STRENGTH.
PHILIPPIANS 4:12-13 NIV

My horse wraps his neck around my shoulders and nickers in my ear. This is how we speak to each other. This is how he says, "I love you." Our friendship is more than just me giving him food and water. My horse is content. He is happy living with me.

What would it take for you to be content—to be happy right where you are? More money, more friends, more stuff? But these things don't last. They will leave us feeling empty and unhappy. The Bible tells us that prizing the things and ideas of this world will pull us away from God (James 4:4). God's Word also tells us to keep our lives free from the love of money and to be content with what we have. That's because money comes and goes, but God "will not leave us or desert us" (Hebrews 13:5 CEV).

We will truly be content only when we know God and follow His plan. It's not a place (or a time in life) we arrive at; it's a choice we can make today.

The apostle Paul was content even during the worst of times. While sharing the gospel, he was shipwrecked, beaten, left for dead, and thrown in prison. In fact, Paul wrote the book of Philippians from a jail cell. How could he be content through all that? Today's verses show that he knew Jesus, and knowing his Savior was enough.

It's so easy to be jealous of people who have more than we do. If we're not careful, those feelings will build up like mold on hay and make us rotten. Remember: the things of this world won't last, but joy and contentment are forever. Trust that God's peace is greater than the world's riches.

LORD, HELP ME BE CONTENT TO LIVE MY LIFE WITH YOU. SHOW ME HOW TO BE JOYFUL, WHETHER I HAVE EVERYTHING OR NOTHING, AMEN.

ONE-OF-A-KIND LOVE

GOD PLANNED FOR US TO DO GOOD THINGS AND TO
LIVE AS HE HAS ALWAYS WANTED US TO LIVE. THAT'S
WHY HE SENT CHRIST TO MAKE US WHAT WE ARE.
EPHESIANS 2:10 CEV

People often ask which of my horses is my favorite. That's like choosing between a hot fudge sundae and a chocolate lava cake! To me, every horse is amazing. And every horse has his or her own special quirks.

For instance, I have a couple of horses that pull their food out of the rack and onto the floor before they eat it. I once met a horse that would eat only green apples, not red ones. And I now own a pony named Cupcake who likes to suck on carrot pieces. Orlando likes to sleep in the same corner of his stall with his head over the automatic waterer, and Grandpa Spike is so old he falls asleep while drinking. When it comes to these four-legged friends, weird is wonderful.

God gave you the gift of being unique too—right down to your fingerprints, your own special talents, and even how you think! God's gifts set you apart from the rest of the herd. Do you love to sing? God has plans to use your voice. Are you a book lover? He planned that too. Does your heart soar when you're outside? He made you that way. Even those things that you think make you odd or different are part of you for a reason. God created you, and He thinks you're wonderful.

God created *you*. He made you with strengths and with weaknesses. He's designed a special plan for your life, listens to your prayers, and has unique ways of helping you grow and learn. The fact that God created us individually also helps us appreciate the special way **He has** made other believers.

Never forget: you are one of a kind. And God loves *you*.

Lord, thank You for making me one of a kind. Help me use my gifts to do the things You planned for me to do, amen.

ALL AROUND YOU

"Therefore I tell you, do not worry about your life, what you will eat or drink; or about your body, what you will wear. . . . Can any one of you by worrying add a single hour to your life?"
Matthew 6:25, 27 niv

One thing I love about horses is that they don't worry. I, however, worry too much. For example, I worry about falling off my horse and breaking my neck. I'm actually allergic to horses (yes, I'm serious). So I worry about whether I packed my eye drops in my saddlebags. I even worry about where to take a bathroom break on the trail.

Maybe you've heard the old saying, "Don't put the cart before the horse." In other words, we worry about something before we even know if it's something to worry about. When we're faced with too little information and too much imagination, we can become our own worst enemies. Anxious thoughts swirl through our brains when we're tired, when we're sick, when we're upset about something else, or when we're late for school. Fear kicks in when our safety is threatened and our circumstances slide out of our control. Suddenly our brains go on full alert, ready to launch into a fight or take flight and run.

Did you know that more than 90 percent of the things we worry about never happen? The truth is, God is protecting us from ourselves. He goes before us, and He guards us from behind: "You are all around me—in front and in back. You have put your hand on me. Your knowledge is amazing to me. It is more than I can understand" (Psalm 139:5–6 icb). Because God is all around us, He knows—and gives us—exactly what we need. Now that's something we can hitch our wagons to.

LORD, HELP ME STOP WORRYING SO MUCH.
GIVE ME THE STRENGTH TO BE CALM AND TO
TRUST THAT YOU ARE IN CONTROL, AMEN.

OUR TRAIL GUIDE

WAIT FOR THE LORD'S HELP. BE STRONG AND
BRAVE, AND WAIT FOR THE LORD'S HELP.
PSALM 27:14 NCV

Horses want our leadership, and more than anything, they *need* it.

Horses that are spoiled because they don't have a strong leader end up upset and unhappy. As you may have seen with some of your own horses, they often act up when they don't feel secure. Those who are too impatient to stand still for mounting can be dangerous. At any moment, an untrained horse may decide to move in the opposite direction, leaving its rider face-first on the ground.

Spoiled. Not feeling safe and secure. Impatient. Sounds familiar, right?

If God didn't lead and train us—if He just gave us everything we wanted the second we wanted it—our faith would be weak. We would think only about ourselves. And the moment something didn't quite go our way, we'd decide that the Lord had abandoned us. (Come to think of it, that isn't faith at all.)

We need the steady guidance of our heavenly Father. He is leading us along the trail and training us to make a difference in the world for Him. Like our horses when we give them a gentle nudge with our heels, we need to move when God calls us to action. When He reins us to the side, we should be prepared to change directions in our lives. When He says, "Not yet," we need to stand patiently at the block and wait until the Lord tells us it's safe to move forward. We can put ourselves in danger if we move in a direction without waiting on God to lead us.

Do you feel God's leading hand on your life? Do you find it hard to be still before Him? Remember: He blesses those who wait on Him. He will lead them exactly where they need to be.

LORD, I WANT YOUR WILL TO BE DONE, NOT MINE. HELP ME TRUST YOU TO LEAD ME. I WILL WAIT PATIENTLY FOR YOU TO SHOW ME THE WAY TO GO, AMEN.

THE NAP SCHEDULE

DEAR FRIENDS, DON'T FORGET THAT FOR THE LORD
ONE DAY IS THE SAME AS A THOUSAND YEARS, AND
A THOUSAND YEARS IS THE SAME AS ONE DAY.
2 PETER 3:8 CEV

You could set a clock to my horse Orlando's afternoon napping schedule. From two to four every afternoon, he's snoozing away in his stall. Since Orlando is an old guy and enjoys his nap routine, I work around his schedule and ride him only in the mornings. Otherwise, he's slow and cranky as we ride.

Most of us enjoy feeling in control of our own schedule. And we get a little cranky when things don't go according to plan. But just like my old horse, we only *think* we are in control. Trusting God to be in control takes a lot of faith and courage. God has perfect timing. *He's never too early and never too late.* He is never in a hurry, but He is always on time.

However, it can be difficult to wait on God's schedule. I don't know about you, but I can be tempted to "help God out" and hurry Him along. In the Old Testament, Sarah got tired of waiting for God to keep His promise to give her and her husband, Abraham, a child. Instead of waiting on God, she decided to hurry God along. That decision created a lot of hurt in Sarah's family (read Genesis 15 and 16).

God isn't a napper. He doesn't take afternoons off. He is always loving, protecting, and blessing us. He is patient with us, giving us every opportunity to come to Him and to be saved. So ask God to help you be patient with His timing. Trust His ways, and don't waste a moment with the Lord.

LORD, I KNOW YOU AREN'T SLOW ABOUT KEEPING
YOUR PROMISES. TEACH ME TO BE PATIENT AND
WAIT ON YOUR PERFECT SCHEDULE, AMEN.

FEAR OR FAITH?

EVEN THOUGH I WALK THROUGH THE DARKEST VALLEY,
I WILL FEAR NO EVIL, FOR YOU ARE WITH ME; YOUR
ROD AND YOUR STAFF, THEY COMFORT ME.
PSALM 23:4 NIV

Horses are prey animals, so they have a fight-or-flight instinct. They will either attack a threat or run from it. At times, this trait can make a trail ride feel more like an adventure on a runaway train. I remember one ride when the combination of noisy farm equipment and a deer spooked my horse several times. I tried to stay calm and cool, but I finally gave up and went home. When our horses spook, it can spook us too. And in those tense moments of fear, we're ready to cut our rides short.

This broken world can make us feel just as spooked. There are days when it's amazing we even have the courage to leave our houses—to face the school day, the bully at lunch, the huge test. *But with God, we have a choice between living in fear and living in faith.* God wants so much more for us than to walk through life full of fear, worry, and anxiety. We may not be in control, but we can trust the One who is.

When fear strikes, the best thing we can do is kneel on those knocking knees. As we go to God in prayer, He gives us peace and comfort. He also provides answers to our prayers and works miracles on our behalf. As we exercise these "trust muscles," they get stronger, and our faith begins to grow.

Try letting go of the reins. Put them into the capable hands of God. You still might spook once in a while, but the closer you get to the Lord, the more fear-proof you'll become.

LORD, CHASE FEAR OUT OF MY LIFE. HELP ME PRAY INSTEAD OF WORRY. AND AS I PRAY, GROW MY FAITH, AMEN.

FOUR-LEGGED HEALERS

THE LORD . . . HEALS THE BROKENHEARTED
AND BANDAGES THEIR WOUNDS.
PSALM 147:2-3 NLT

God brings horses into our lives when He knows we need them most—whether we are lonely or deep in sadness. In moments of weakness, horses encourage us and build us up. I have a horse named Rethel who helped a teenage girl mend a heart bruised by bad friends. A pony named Charlie Brown helped another young person's heart heal from bullying. Orlando, one of my horses, took my mind off some health struggles.

But no matter how amazing horses are, complete healing comes only from the Father.

God will bring the right verses, worship songs, and people into our lives when He knows we need them most. When we are lonely or upset, *He will send us His love in creative ways*—like a kiss from a puppy, a text from a friend, or even a line from a book or movie. As we learn to trust Him to comfort us, we learn to go to His side more and more.

So when we feel beaten down by hurtful people, sin, and events in our lives we can't control, we can take our pain to God. He will mend our brokenness. In fact, Scripture tells us the Lord will give us back our joy: "You will teach me how to live a holy life. Being with you will fill me with joy; at your right hand I will find pleasure forever" (Psalm 16:11 NCV).

There are some things we can't fix on our own. They can only be mended by the loving-kindness of the Savior. Trust His healing work.

Lord, the Bible says You heal the brokenhearted and bandage up their wounds. I need Your healing touch. Bring peace and joy to my heart, amen.

A LITTLE HELP
AROUND THE BARN

"The Helper will teach you everything and will cause you to remember all that I told you. This Helper is the Holy Spirit whom the Father will send in my name."
JOHN 14:26 NCV

It's nice to have help around the barn. Stable hands look after horses' everyday needs. They make sure the animals are healthy and in good condition.

We, too, have Someone to help us and encourage us to live our best. The third person of the Trinity—the Holy Spirit—is our Guide and Helper. He gives us strength and prays to the Father for us. The Holy Spirit was sent by God to live in us and give us direction in every part of our daily lives. Jesus said, "I will ask the Father, and he will give you another Helper to be with you forever" (John 14:16 NCV). Like the Father and the Son, God the Holy Spirit is Someone we should believe and obey.

Being filled with the Spirit results in a rich and full life. Before I invited the Holy Spirit to work in my life, I felt like the world around me was dull and gray. I had all the things that were *supposed* to make me happy, but they didn't. I found myself asking, "Is this all there is?"

The Holy Spirit is God's hand working in my life. If we are willing to listen and obey, the Holy Spirit will guide us to the plan God has for our lives. I experience the life that God has planned for me as the Spirit opens doors of blessings and closes doors to things that would harm me. It's a life of highs and lows, but it's always in rich color.

If you're looking for a life that's a bit more full, start walking in the Spirit today.

LORD, FILL ME WITH YOUR HOLY SPIRIT AND GUIDE MY STEPS. HELP ME LIVE MY LIFE IN COLOR WITH YOU, AMEN.

A JUICY TIDBIT

GOSSIPS CAN'T KEEP SECRETS, SO AVOID
PEOPLE WHO TALK TOO MUCH.
PROVERBS 20:19 NCV

Do you ever wonder what horses talk about as they gather around the hay bale? Perhaps they're chatting about a juicy tidbit of gossip that's going around the barn.

If you've ever heard the latest gossip around the lunch table, you know it's tempting to join in. That's because it's part of our sinful nature to build ourselves up by tearing others down. We need God's help to tame our tongues. God compared the tongue to poison (James 3:8) because He knows how much harm words can do. In Psalm 141:3, David prayed, "Help me control my tongue. Help me be careful about what I say" (ICB).

Gossip can ruin friendships, damage reputations, and make trusting others difficult. It's always best to avoid someone who gossips. And if you are the one who is gossiping, ask God to help you bridle your tongue.

Just imagine how much good we could do for God if we learned to control our tongues. The Bible teaches that our words also have the power to strengthen others. Instead of using words that hurt, use words that will help heal the wounds of others. Proverbs is full of verses about being careful with your words—check out Proverbs 17:9 and Proverbs 26:20. Memorize these verses and remember them when you're tempted to gossip.

I'm convinced that if we love our neighbors like Jesus asked us to do (Matthew 22:39), then we are loving like a horse does. And that means we are encouraging others and building them up—not gossiping or tearing them down.

LORD, TAME MY TONGUE. TEACH ME TO USE WORDS THAT HEAL, NOT THOSE THAT HURT. HELP ME NOT TO GOSSIP, AMEN.

THE ESCAPE ARTIST

YOU SURELY KNOW THAT YOUR BODY IS A TEMPLE WHERE
THE HOLY SPIRIT LIVES. THE SPIRIT IS IN YOU AND IS
A GIFT FROM GOD. YOU ARE NO LONGER YOUR OWN.
1 CORINTHIANS 6:19 CEV

My Shetland pony, Tucker, can open almost any door with his lips. Although it's extremely cute, this troublesome skill could lead Tucker into a serious situation. That's why I put locks on the doors that lead to possible danger. Just because Tucker *can* do something doesn't mean he *should*.

That's true of us as well. Even when something isn't against the rules, that doesn't mean it's good for us. The Bible says our bodies are a gift from God. We are temples, or homes, of the Holy Spirit. That's why we should use our bodies to honor Him.

Think about what you do each day with your body: talk, eat, exercise. Now ask God, "Is everything I do something You want for my life? Does it help me live a holy life? Or does it pull me away from You?"

If some of your daily choices are wrong, don't get stuck in shame. Simply confess your sin and ask the Father to help you do better. The truth is, no one is born holy. Only God can bring holiness into our lives.

However, the more we try to please God in all that we do, the more we'll begin to think as He thinks and become the holy people He wants us to be. We'll become more likely to choose things that make our faith stronger. Our holiness is possible only because Jesus died on the cross.

He breathes His own holiness into our lives, and He will present us as holy to the Father.

Lord, I know my body is a temple of the Holy Spirit. I know I belong to You. I was bought at a price—the price of Jesus dying on the cross. Teach me to honor You with my body. Teach me to be holy as You are holy, amen.

MORE THAN YOU CAN IMAGINE

WITH GOD'S POWER WORKING IN US, GOD CAN DO MUCH, MUCH MORE THAN ANYTHING WE CAN ASK OR IMAGINE. TO HIM BE GLORY IN THE CHURCH AND IN CHRIST JESUS FOR ALL TIME, FOREVER AND EVER. AMEN.
EPHESIANS 3:20–21 NCV

Just when we think God can't make horses any better, He goes a little further and gives us the therapy horse. If you have ever had the privilege of seeing these horses in action, you would know the care God takes when He knits each one of them together. Through the use of therapy horses, some children take their first steps and speak their first words. These horses give many people the strength to live amazing lives.

Some of the people whose lives will be changed most by therapy horses are reluctant to approach the animal at first. Gradually, these folks begin to understand and develop a relationship with the horses.

In the same way, some people are reluctant to approach God. Often it's because they're afraid or they misunderstand who He is. These people become so bogged down with wrong ideas about what they think Christianity is that they miss out on having a relationship with God.

Sometimes we have to step out of our comfort zones in order to learn something new—especially to discover how amazing God is. The great promise to those who seek the Lord is that He will be found. But we must take the time to seek Him for ourselves: "You will seek me and find me when you seek me with all your heart" (Jeremiah 29:13 NIV).

God goes beyond our expectations—just as He did on the cross and at Jesus' resurrection. God goes further than we could ever imagine and keeps amazing us with His goodness.

LORD, I THANK YOU FOR BEING THERE WHEN I
SEARCH FOR YOU. AND I PRAISE YOU FOR GOING
WAY BEYOND MY EXPECTATIONS, AMEN.

TOO GOOD TO BE TRUE

"THEN YOU WILL KNOW THE TRUTH, AND THE TRUTH WILL MAKE YOU FREE."
JOHN 8:32 NCV

There is no such thing as a startle-proof horse. Although certain horses are more trustworthy than others, all horses are still prey animals. You can't guarantee a horse won't react to a situation with the fight-or-flight response God gave him. No matter what you are told about a horse, promises about behavior are too good to be true. Wherever and whenever you ride, always wear your helmet.

As Christians, we sometimes hear things that are too good to be true. Some preachers sell the lie that a mixture of positive speech, good thoughts, faith that never asks questions, and large gifts of money will improve your health, your finances, and your whole life. According to these leaders, your new Christian life will be hunky-dory. Friends, the fantasy of a pain-free life is too good to be true. If these teachers decided to be honest about their teachings, their motto would read, "We can catch a fly with honey, and we catch even more with a pile of horse manure."

The fact is, bad things happen to godly people all the time. Our Savior never guaranteed us a pain-free life, and He loves us too much to promise that we won't have to face hard times. With each trouble, God shows us where our faith is weak. He draws us closer to Himself and His grace. A flood brings flowers, a surgeon's scalpel brings healing, and a crucifixion brought salvation. Blessings can be both bitter and sweet at the same time.

This world is guaranteed to buck you off and probably kick you around a little too. So put on your helmet. Trials and troubles remind us that our true home is with God in heaven. Count it all joy. The best is yet to come.

LORD, HELP ME TELL THE TRUTH FROM LIES.
GIVE ME YOUR STRENGTH WHEN HARD TIMES
COME. HELP ME COUNT IT ALL JOY, AMEN.

A BIG, HAPPY NEIGH

ENCOURAGE EACH OTHER EVERY DAY WHILE IT IS
"TODAY." HELP EACH OTHER SO NONE OF YOU WILL
BECOME HARDENED BECAUSE SIN HAS TRICKED YOU.
HEBREWS 3:13 NCV

Nothing is more encouraging than when my horse neighs to me from across the pasture. That big neigh is a happy noise that makes me feel like I'm his favorite person.

In contrast, I once met a grumpy, weathered old horse trainer who always had an insulting remark for people who hand-fed treats to their horses. He told those of us who kissed our horses, "You're spoiling them." While I agreed that hand-feeding treats makes for pushy horses, there was no way I was going to stop puckering up for my pony. Then one day, when he thought no one was looking, this same cowboy kissed his horse on the nose.

Some say our character is shown by how we treat others when no one else is looking. Like that weathered old cowboy, why do we sometimes hide our pleasant side and show the ugly one instead? As a human, you will want to be unkind at times. But you don't have to act on it. Next time you feel tempted to show the world your mean streak, make a surprising change and do the opposite by saying something positive.

When we don't have encouragement in our lives, we feel unloved, unimportant, useless, and forgotten. A kind word (or a big neigh), however, can make our day. *Encouragement is a simple and thoughtful gift, and it doesn't cost you a thing.* If you're kind when everyone is looking, you will soon be known as a great encourager, and your example will help others do the same.

This world is filled with plenty of grumpy old "nay"sayers. Choose to be a "neigh"sayer instead, and let people around you know their value.

LORD, PLEASE GIVE ME AN OPPORTUNITY TO ENCOURAGE SOMEONE TODAY. LET MY WORDS SOFTEN A HARDENED HEART, AMEN.

WAITING FOR THE SHOE TO DROP

THEREFORE DO NOT WORRY ABOUT TOMORROW,
FOR TOMORROW WILL WORRY ABOUT ITSELF. EACH
DAY HAS ENOUGH TROUBLE OF ITS OWN.
MATTHEW 6:34 NIV

W e put a lot of faith in our farriers—those people who put the shoes on our horses. But as our trail ride gets closer, some of us question whether our horses' shoes are solidly in place. Some people spend their whole ride missing the scenery because they are anxiously looking down, waiting for a shoe to drop.

What about you? When good things happen in your life, do you joyfully delight in those moments and God's blessings? Or are you left with the feeling that now something bad will happen to mess it all up? Do you enjoy playing on the team, or worry about making the next out? Do you celebrate the good grade, or worry about the next test?

"Waiting for the other shoe to drop" is another way of saying "letting the devil steal our joy." Waiting for something bad to happen in our lives can leave us feeling constantly anxious and living in fear. If you find yourself ending friendships before people have a chance to hurt you, or if you are asking God to just get your next big disappointment over with, then the devil has stolen your joy.

It is true, sometimes we lose a shoe. Sometimes we lose the whole horse. But by being afraid of the things that *could* happen, you are missing the joys that come in the in-between moments. Between major disappointments and major blessings, joyfully live your life. When worry and fear creep in, make a list of all the good things that happen to you in just one day—family, meals, this book, and of course, your shoes.

Don't wait for the next shoe to drop. Instead, thank God for the blessings you have right now. When we focus on the bad stuff, we miss the ways that God is caring for us all the time. Embrace the journey with God. Choose joy.

LORD, FORGIVE ME FOR WORRYING INSTEAD
OF ENJOYING YOUR BLESSINGS. BE CLOSE
TO ME AND GIVE ME PEACE, AMEN.

EXPECT THE UNEXPECTED

I WAIT PATIENTLY FOR GOD TO SAVE
ME. ONLY HE GIVES ME HOPE.
PSALM 62:5 ICB

If you look around a "horses for sale" website, it seems every other ad features a horse that's "child-safe," "calm," or "won't buck or bite." But no horse is perfect.

I wish people would do right by their horses and sell them with honesty. Sadly, when these falsely advertised horses fail us, the new owners remember the lies they read in the ad. If we have formed expectations about horses that they cannot live up to, it is not their fault.

Just as there are no perfect horses, there are no perfect churches, families, or friends. Expecting too much from others can get us into trouble. When we expect perfection out of people or situations, it is not their fault. Rather, our crushed hopes are the result of our own flawed expectations.

The good news is that you have the power to change your expectations by simply changing your attitude. When the disciples obediently followed Jesus back to Jerusalem, they fully expected Jesus to be crowned their military king. Peter, James, John, and the other apostles believed Jesus would throw out the Romans, who had taken over the Jewish people and their lands. When the Son of Man was arrested, tried, and nailed to a cross instead, the disciples were heartbroken.

Because the Messiah failed to live up to what they had expected, the disciples missed the greatest victory of all time: the resurrection. Today, God is still crushing the expectations of those who think they have it all figured out. But He is also continually blessing the humble in ways they never saw coming.

Thankfully, Jesus turns His kingdom upside down all the time by doing things differently than you or I would. ***God is mighty—and He's mighty good at surprising us.*** So instead of slinking off in disappointment and turning tail when God doesn't do what you expect, humbly make your way over to God. He will surprise you in glorious ways.

LORD, FORGIVE ME FOR EXPECTING YOU TO
WORK IN HUMAN WAYS. GIVE ME EYES TO
SEE YOUR GLORIOUS PLANS, AMEN.

X-RAYING EVERYTHING

SATAN CHANGES HIMSELF TO LOOK LIKE AN ANGEL
OF LIGHT. SO IT DOES NOT SURPRISE US IF SATAN'S
SERVANTS ALSO MAKE THEMSELVES LOOK LIKE
SERVANTS WHO WORK FOR WHAT IS RIGHT. BUT IN THE
END THEY WILL BE PUNISHED FOR WHAT THEY DO.
2 CORINTHIANS 11:14–15 NCV

Lameness is a horse's most common injury. A lame horse doesn't walk naturally. And it's often impossible to see what the problem is without an X-ray. I've owned a few horses that needed X-rays. Most of them had something that needed "stall rest" for a few days, and they recovered fine. But one horse named Banner was lame because of a disease in his bones. Because we found it early, Banner got the treatment he needed and got better.

Sometimes we need spiritual X-rays. Satan will try to disguise himself and make it look as if he stands for something good. It takes wisdom to see the evil that needs to be dealt with.

I have learned to X-ray everything under the light of God's Word. For example, the travel ball team sounds great . . . until you see that games are on Sunday mornings. And that new friend seems wonderful . . . until she encourages you to lie.

When new activities, friendships, or opportunities come our way, we should pray about them and see what the Bible has to say. Ask a grown-up to help you find verses to point you in the right direction. Today, we have so many great tools to help us understand God's truth. Why not ask your parents for a study Bible—one that's made just for your age? Then read a bit of it daily. Read Psalms or the gospel of John if you're unsure where to start.

Don't let Satan get you off track. When you know more of the Bible, the Holy Spirit will remind you of key verses as you go about your day. If you're willing to put in the work, God's Word will show you the truth and keep you spiritually strong.

LORD, TEACH ME TO BE WISE AND NOT TO LET THE ENEMY FOOL ME. KEEP ME IN THE LIGHT OF YOUR TRUTH, AMEN.

THE MISSING PIECE

WHEN I FELT MY FEET SLIPPING, YOU CAME
WITH YOUR LOVE AND KEPT ME STEADY.
PSALM 94:18 CEV

Have you ever been on a saddle that was slipping because the girth strap—the one that goes under the horse's body—wasn't tight enough? You try to keep your balance by shifting to one side or the other. But if you're not careful, you'll go over the side and end up on the ground.

God's love is like that girth strap. It holds you in place and keeps you balanced in life. Without it, life is wobbly. Before I knew the Lord, it seemed as if I had everything a person could want. I had a great family, great friends, and nice things—but something was lacking. I tried first one thing and then another, searching for the missing piece in my life.

It took me a long time to realize *God was that missing piece.* Slowly, I began to believe in the healing power of Jesus Christ. As it turns out, the whole time I was looking for that missing piece, God was chasing after me.

Don't let anyone tell you that God doesn't care about the little details of your life. God is interested in *everything* that happens to us. No worry is too big or too small for His attention. When we give God our problems, He promises to give us peace so complete that we can't understand it. What God wants most is a relationship with *you.* Find your balance and your "missing piece" in Him. He'll hold you tight and keep you right-side up.

Lord, when I feel as if I'm slipping, I need
Your love to hold me fast, amen.

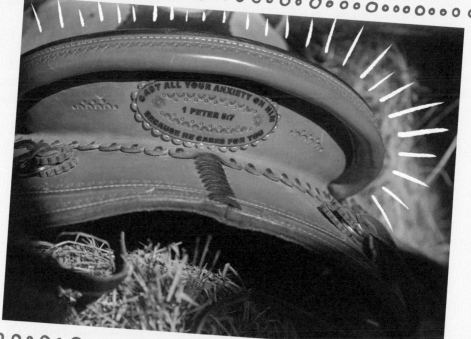

IT TAKES TIME

WITHOUT FAITH NO ONE CAN PLEASE GOD. ANYONE WHO
COMES TO GOD MUST BELIEVE THAT HE IS REAL AND THAT
HE REWARDS THOSE WHO TRULY WANT TO FIND HIM.
HEBREWS 11:6 NCV

Sometimes the bond between horse and owner needs time to build. My best relationships with horses are the ones that didn't come easily. Just when I would have my doubts about whether we were going to work out, I would get a response from my horse that would draw us closer together.

I once owned a Fjord horse named Gus. When he first came to my farm, Gus was very naughty. I thought I made a huge mistake by getting him. But over time, we learned to trust each other, and we started to have small successes. Eventually, he figured out I was worth trusting and that I would keep him safe.

I'd say that almost all of us struggle with trusting God sometimes. The best cure for that is faith. And faith comes by studying the Word of God and being in His presence day in and day out.

I study and spend time with God in a variety of ways. I enjoy listening to a lot of sermons. I also love telling others about Jesus, and I believe God has called me to do this. When I talk to others about what Jesus Christ has done in my life and what He can do in theirs, that builds my faith. I also speak to God and ask Him what He wants me to do to serve Him. I read the Bible and do Bible studies (right now I am doing a study on Jonah). I attend church on Sundays and use Bible apps to learn more about His Word.

When you draw near to God, He will draw even nearer to you in response. Day by day, your relationship with Him will build. It doesn't come easily, but trust me—it will be worth the effort.

LORD, STRENGTHEN MY FAITH AND HELP ME WHEN
I DON'T TRUST YOU COMPLETELY. I PRAISE YOU
FOR BEING MY LORD AND SAVIOR, AMEN.

YOU CAN'T FOOL
A HORSE

NOTHING IN ALL THE WORLD CAN BE HIDDEN FROM GOD.
EVERYTHING IS CLEAR AND LIES OPEN BEFORE HIM. AND
TO HIM WE MUST EXPLAIN THE WAY WE HAVE LIVED.
HEBREWS 4:13 ICB

Horses pick up on the feelings of the people around them. When we are upset, they sense how we are feeling. You cannot fool a horse. They are great judges of character and moods.

We can't fool God either. It's impossible to get anything past Him. In the garden of Eden, Adam and Eve tried to hide from God after they disobeyed His commands. God knew exactly what they'd been up to, of course. And He knew where they were. Still He called out, "Where are you?" and came looking for them.

That story is good news for us. Even when we've messed up, God doesn't stop chasing after us. He searches for us in our messes and mistakes because He loves us—no matter what we've done.

Why do we try to hide from God? He already knows where we are and what we've done. He knows our moods and our doubts, our struggles and our troubles. He knows who we really are and what we can do—both the good and the bad.

Just as God went looking for Adam and Eve, He's looking for you. He *wants* to be with you. He's more than ready to hear you and forgive you. When your sin weighs you down, confess it to God. When you truly repent, God will always give you His mercy and forgiveness.

LORD, FORGIVE ME FOR HIDING FROM YOU WHEN I SIN. I PRAISE YOU FOR YOUR MERCY. HEAR MY CONFESSION AND CLEANSE MY HEART OF SIN, AMEN.

NO FAVORITES

In Christ, there is no difference between Jew
and Greek, slave and free person, male and
female. You are all the same in Christ Jesus.
GALATIANS 3:28 NCV

Filly or colt, buckskin or black, Shetland or Arabian? There are countless varieties of horses in the world, and there are many opinions on which breed or color is best. Thankfully, horses don't care much about the outside appearance of people. Horses will faithfully carry us, no matter how much money we have, what color our skin is, or whether we're a guy or a girl. We are each truly equal in their eyes.

Every believer has equal standing in God's eyes too. As we read in the book of Acts, Jews and Gentiles worshiped together for the first time in the early church. The mixing of people who were used to being separate caused a lot of issues. In his letters, Paul made it clear that they were all in the gospel-preaching business together. No longer would Jews and Gentiles worship God separately. Instead, they would learn the same stories and share the same cup and bread. I'm sure some of those believers were horrified by the freedom Paul preached. They simply weren't used to the life-changing nature of God's grace.

Today, we still tend to separate ourselves into groups. Think about your church, school, and friend groups. Do homeschooling families look down on public schoolers? Do the sports kids make fun of band kids? Do band kids make fun of horse kids? Maybe you've been guilty of judging how much someone loves God by the way they look.

When we look down on a person, we are hurting someone God created in His own image, someone He loves deeply. And we are hurting somebody Jesus died for. God does not play favorites, and neither should we.

LORD, THANK YOU FOR SEEING ME AS EQUAL TO OTHERS. THANK YOU THAT ALL BELIEVERS ARE THE SAME IN JESUS CHRIST, AMEN.

A SOFT HEART

"BLESSED ARE THE PURE IN HEART, FOR THEY WILL SEE GOD."
MATTHEW 5:8 NIV

When I was about fourteen years old, my horse Roanie got brain cancer. Losing Roanie made me so sad that I vowed never to grow close to another horse again. Then, many years later, the barn my daughter rode at offered to sell me one of their horses. When I thought about it, I realized I was missing out on life by keeping my heart from horses. I then purchased Orlando.

When I softened my heart to the idea that I could ride again, it opened my life to so many new experiences and friendships. A soft heart feels more pain—but it also experiences more life.

God's Word is clear that we need soft hearts to follow Him. Years ago, any Christian crossing my path would have thought my heart was hard and untouchable. But one day, I read the words Jesus said on the cross: "Father, forgive them, for they do not know what they are doing" (Luke 23:34 NIV). These words softened my heart. They helped me hear the truth that I, too, could be forgiven.

We all have people in our lives who are running away from God. It may seem like a waste of time to pray for these unbelievers and their hard hearts. But that's when we should pray even harder. After Jesus prayed for His enemies that day on the cross, a hardened criminal found forgiveness and a Roman centurion recognized Jesus as the Son of God.

Pray for unbelievers to soften their hearts to God. And pray for your heart to remain soft to the Holy Spirit and all the joys God wants to give you.

LORD, HELP ME KEEP A SOFT HEART TOWARD YOU AND ALL THE JOYS YOU WANT TO GIVE ME, AMEN.

LIVE FREE

We have freedom now, because Christ made us free. So stand strong. Do not change and go back into the slavery of the law.
GALATIANS 5:1 NCV

The idea of horses living free in the wild is a wonderful thought, indeed. But the truth is, all wild horses need human help to survive. Finding food and water and staying away from roaring mountain lions are just some of the worries "free" horses have that our barn horses do not. In other words, a life full of worry, fear, and death is not a way to live free at all.

Those who don't follow Christ often talk about how free they are. But living outside God's Word—and paying the price for sin—is anything but freedom. It's slavery.

Think of that kid who does whatever she pleases, no matter what happens. She pushes to the front of the line. She's quick to take the best for herself—the best seat, best snack, best everything. Pretty soon she'll find herself sitting alone because no one wants to hang out with someone like that. Or think about that guy who makes fun of others behind their backs—even his friends—because he thinks it's funny. But one day, when he really needs his friends, they won't be there.

Does that sound like living free to you? Not at all. The truth is, God gave us the Bible, and He commands us to obey the words in it in order to protect us. He knows us better than we know ourselves, and He wants to give us what we truly long for: to be loved no matter what and to have a purpose for our lives.

True freedom comes from knowing Christ and living by His Word. Trust Him to guide you in ways that are best for you. Live free.

LORD, I PRAISE YOU FOR THE FREEDOM FROM SIN AND DEATH YOU GIVE TO EVERYONE WHO GIVES HIS OR HER LIFE TO YOU. HELP ME SEE THAT LIVING FREE ONLY HAPPENS WHEN I'M LIVING WITH YOU, AMEN.

RIGHT WHERE YOU ARE

SITTING DOWN, JESUS CALLED THE TWELVE AND
SAID, "ANYONE WHO WANTS TO BE FIRST MUST BE
THE VERY LAST, AND THE SERVANT OF ALL."
MARK 9:35 NIV

E very foal born on my farm is full of possibilities. Of course, my dreams for them are always much bigger than reality. In my heart, they are all World Cup winners, and that includes my donkeys!

In the same way, every child born on this planet has dreams—dreams that can be much bigger than how their lives actually turn out. Ask your friends what they want to be when they grow up, and the options are endless. From becoming the president of the United States to the scientist who cures cancer, there are so many possibilities. However, there are few who pick "service" as a dream job.

Because we serve such a mighty God, we make the mistake of thinking everything He wants us to do for Him must be done on a huge scale. But that's not always the case. *God puts us in the places where we will do the most good for Him.* And that could be in a store sweeping floors or in a barn cleaning out stalls.

Charles Spurgeon was a famous preacher—so famous that he is called the "Prince of Preachers." But he never went to college. In fact, his first lessons about God were from a lunch lady. Thanks to this perfectly placed, servant-hearted woman, the Prince of Preachers grew up to change the world. Whose heart might you touch where God has placed you?

Do you think you can't serve God because you are "only a _____"? What would God say? God knows everything, and He sees unlimited possibilities in each of us to help people learn about Christ right where we are. You might never know (this side of heaven) the difference you have made. After all, your life on earth is just the beginning. And God's plans are much bigger and better than we can imagine.

LORD, MAKE ME A SERVANT. USE ME TO TELL OTHERS ABOUT YOU, WHEREVER YOU PLACE ME, AMEN.

BIT VERSUS BITLESS

YOU ARE JOINED TOGETHER WITH PEACE THROUGH THE SPIRIT,
SO MAKE EVERY EFFORT TO CONTINUE TOGETHER IN THIS WAY.
EPHESIANS 4:3 NCV

As much as I enjoy horses, there have been a few I've had a hard time loving. If I were to judge all horses by these few, I would miss out on the joyful bonds I have with the horses who adore me. People, like horses, come in all types. Some of them are harder to love than others. And the things we disagree on can bring out the difficult-to-love parts of all of us.

One place you'll see this happen is in an argument you find in the horse world: whether it's best to use a bridle with or without a bit. The *bit* is the piece of metal or plastic that goes in the horse's mouth and helps the rider guide the horse. I do not consider myself "horse smart" enough to give a good opinion on the bit-versus-bitless argument. But plenty of horse people will tell you what they think. And sometimes these strong opinions lead to name-calling and anger.

Why are we so hard to get along with at times? What makes us think we have the right answer about things like horse bits? When we get frustrated by things we can't control, we can lose control of ourselves.

Every time we go on the internet or step outside our bedrooms, there's the possibility of running into difficult people (and becoming difficult ourselves). We can't change others or their choices. Trying to control people is like trying to bridle the wind. But we can choose our own behaviors and what to do when we disagree with others. We can also pray to see people as God sees them.

This world is full of all types of human beings. Don't let a few difficult folks rob you of the joy of healthy friendships with lovely people.

LORD, HELP ME SEE PEOPLE AS YOU DO. GIVE ME PATIENCE AROUND DIFFICULT PEOPLE, AMEN.

"HELLO"

"THIS, THEN, IS HOW YOU SHOULD PRAY."
MATTHEW 6:9 NIV

Most of us won't remember the first conversation we had with our horses, but it had to have started with some form of "Hello." I like to say hello with a brush. Brushing horses builds trust between human and horse. Brushing makes the horse—and you—calm. It's my favorite language to use with horses as we grow closer.

One of the best ways to grow closer to God is to speak to Him in prayer. It doesn't have to be long or fancy. Prayer is simply a conversation with God.

However, if you feel like you don't know what to say or how to say it, you're not alone. Lots of new believers (and even faithful people who've believed for a long time) feel that same way.

The disciples admired the miracles Jesus did and the comfortable way He talked with God. So they asked Him to teach them to pray. That's why Jesus gave us the Lord's Prayer (Matthew 6:9–13). It's an excellent outline for prayer.

The prayer begins with praise: "May your name always be kept holy" (Matthew 6:9 NCV). Beginning our prayers with praise gets us in the right frame of mind. Next, Jesus humbly surrendered to God and declared that He wanted what God wanted: "May your kingdom come, and what you want be done" (v. 10 NCV). The prayer then asks for the daily things we need and for mercy: "Give us the food we need for each day. Forgive us for our sins" (v. 11–12 NCV). It ends by asking God to guide and protect His children.

There is nothing wrong with reading and saying a prayer written by others. Just make sure whatever you say, it comes from your heart.

God is listening. He longs for a relationship with you. So don't wait. Start the conversation by simply saying, "Hello."

LORD, THANK YOU FOR EXAMPLES OF POWERFUL AND EFFECTIVE PRAYER. TEACH ME TO PRAY, AMEN.

REAL TRAILERING

THE FAITHFUL LOVE OF THE Lord NEVER ENDS! HIS
MERCIES NEVER CEASE. GREAT IS HIS FAITHFULNESS;
HIS MERCIES BEGIN AFRESH EACH MORNING.
LAMENTATIONS 3:22–23 NLT

I would confidently pull a horse trailer all day long if the road I traveled was guaranteed to be straight and free of dangers. But real trailering involves lots of backing up, sudden stops, and winding roads.

Living a Christian life doesn't guarantee straight paths either. Because we live in a fallen world, each of us is sure to have times when we need to back up and start over or stop suddenly. We'll hit speed bumps that slow us down. Even after deciding to follow Christ, we are still sinners who aren't free from the temptation to sin. ***Becoming a Christian doesn't make you perfect; it just makes you saved.*** Thankfully, God has promised never to let you be tempted beyond what you can stand (1 Corinthians 10:13). He will make a way out of that temptation so you can escape sin.

Your journey with Christ most certainly will not be a straight line. Rather, it will have plenty of twists and turns and dangers. You'll be forced at times to back up and try again, learning from your mistakes. Yet, if you mess up royally and break one of His laws, God promises to forgive you if you confess with a heart that is truly sorry.

I don't know about you, but I'm glad God is with me on life's road trip. Through all the twists and turns, we can be sure that God surrounds us with His faithful love.

Lord, thank You for always loving me.
Thank You for not letting me be tempted
beyond what I can stand, amen.

NEVER ALONE

"YOU CAN BE SURE THAT I WILL BE WITH YOU ALWAYS. I WILL
CONTINUE WITH YOU UNTIL THE END OF THE WORLD."
MATTHEW 28:20 ICB

Horses want companionship—and they require it. Relying on each other helps horses feel safe. As prey animals, they want an extra set of eyes to help watch for predators. You may have noticed that lone horses are often depressed.

Just as horses need companionship, so do people. We all need someone to talk to, but sometimes we feel alone. Sometimes we feel lonely even when we are not by ourselves. *There's a big lie the devil wants you to believe: you are all alone.* All of us—at least once in our lives—end up believing this lie. Satan's goal is to make us feel alone and unimportant. He wants us to see our problems as evidence that God has abandoned us or that we are unlovable.

However, we don't have to play the devil's game. Let your feelings spur you to make a positive change. Instead of running from your loneliness or pretending it's not real, use it to let God in. Remind yourself that God is with you and for you. Before He rose up to heaven after His resurrection, Jesus said, "I am with you always." He did not say "sometimes" or "only on Sundays." He said *always*, and He meant it.

You are not alone in this life, so don't choose to go at it alone. Invite Jesus into your heart. He will be the Friend who is closer than a brother, and He wants to show you the purpose He has for you. God has a plan for your life, and it's a good one. Let God fill up your lonely places by accepting His love today.

LORD, I SOMETIMES FEEL LONELY, BUT THANK YOU
FOR NEVER LEAVING ME. REMIND ME OF YOUR
PRESENCE WHENEVER I FEEL ALONE, AMEN.

SHAKEN UP

> "I KNOW WHAT I AM PLANNING FOR YOU," SAYS THE
> LORD. "I HAVE GOOD PLANS FOR YOU, NOT PLANS TO HURT
> YOU. I WILL GIVE YOU HOPE AND A GOOD FUTURE."
> JEREMIAH 29:11 NCV

It's rare, but occasionally my horse Sven gets loose. The perfect combination of tall, green grass and a hole in the fencing is just too great a temptation for him to pass up. Even though Sven thinks he's happier grazing in the ditch by the road, it's a dangerous place. So I shake a bucket of grain to get his attention, and he follows me back to the safety of the barn.

Like me with that bucket of grain, God shakes up our lives to get our attention when we start trusting that false sense of happiness the world provides. A while back, I had a great job and an amazing family. We had no worries about money or our home. So where was God going to shake things up? With my health.

I had planted an orchard of fruit trees—and then I couldn't eat fruit. God even took away my ability to drink *coffee*, which is my favorite! By taking away the one thing I really had no control over, my health, God got my attention. In that frustrating time, I moved from being just a Jesus believer to a Jesus *follower*. I began actually having a relationship with my Creator. I wasn't in control of any of it, and I realized I didn't want to be.

God is a loving Father. He shakes the bucket to protect His children, not to upset, hurt, or punish them. He wants to lead us back to the safety of the specific path He has for each of us.

Lord, shake up my life and do whatever You need to do to keep me on the path toward You. I know that lasting happiness can be found only in a deeper relationship with You, amen.

THE GOOD NEWS

GIVE THANKS TO THE LORD AND PROCLAIM HIS GREATNESS.
LET THE WHOLE WORLD KNOW WHAT HE HAS DONE.
PSALM 105:1 NLT

There are so many good things that come from having horses. Still, I've had moments when I had to deal with bad news. Horse injuries, serious illnesses, and loss of life are unfortunate lessons that come with owning horses.

The only benefit of bad news is that it helps us appreciate the good news.

As Christians, we hear a lot about the good news, but sometimes we don't hear about the bad. The thing is that we can't have the good news without the bad. The bad news is that we are all sinners. If we say we have no sin, we lie to ourselves. But if we understand that we are headed for hell without Jesus' forgiveness of our sin, we can appreciate all that He did for us on the cross.

Our loving Lord took onto Himself the punishment for our sin when He died on the cross. Every day we choose to disobey some of God's commands. If God gave us the punishment we deserve, we would die in our sin and be separated from Him forever. However, God wants to have a relationship with us, and He wants to spend eternity with us. That's why He sent Jesus to live a perfect life and take our punishment by dying a horrible death. He died in our place so that we don't have to be judged for our sins.

Once you recognize that you are a sinner, you can accept Jesus, your Savior. Then the bad news turns to good, and you can't help sharing the gospel (which means "good news") with others.

Heaven is not for good people. Heaven is for forgiven people.

LORD, THANK YOU FOR BEING FAITHFUL AND JUST AND FOR FORGIVING MY SINS. GIVE ME THE COURAGE TO SHARE YOUR GOOD NEWS WITH THE PEOPLE I MEET EVERY DAY, AMEN.

BARN CHORES

"FATHER, IF YOU ARE WILLING, TAKE AWAY THIS CUP OF
SUFFERING. BUT DO WHAT YOU WANT, NOT WHAT I WANT."
LUKE 22:42 NCV

No matter what the weather is like—steamy hot, freezing cold, or pouring down rain—horses have to be fed. That means we horse owners have to get out of our comfy homes and head off to the barn.

On days when the weather is harsh and unforgiving, we still have to get our chores done. As humans, it's in our nature to try to get the biggest result with the least amount of effort. If there were any possible way to get our barn chores done from the warmth of our homes, we would do it. But because we love our horses and there is no other way, we buck up, gear up, and do our chores the best we can.

In the Garden of Gethsemane, Jesus prayed to His Father three times, asking, "Father . . . take away this cup of suffering." Jesus was fully God, but He was also fully human in every way. His human nature was perfect, but He was still battling to accept the torture and the shame He knew waited for Him on the cross. In other words, He was asking His Father if there was any other way.

Out of His love for us and His obedience to God, Jesus willingly gave up His life when He went to the cross to die for us. Jesus took the hardest way possible to narrow our road down to two choices: we can either accept Him into our lives as our Savior, or we can decide to live apart from God.

Jesus is the *only* way to God and the *only* way to heaven. Accept Him into your life today, and then share Him with others.

Lord, forgive me for sometimes choosing the easy path over the best path. Thank You for Jesus, who sets the best example for me, amen.

THE PONY EXPRESS

HE SAID TO THEM, "GO INTO ALL THE WORLD AND
PREACH THE GOSPEL TO ALL CREATION."
MARK 16:15 NIV

In the mid-1800s, three creative men brainstormed and came up with a plan to allow mail to reach long distances quickly—by riders traveling on horseback. According to HistoryNet, "The lack of speedy communication between the mid-west and the west was [made even worse] by the looming threat of a civil war. Russell, Waddell and Majors designed a system that spanned . . . over one hundred stations, each approximately two hundred forty miles [apart], across the country."[2]

The Pony Express, as it came to be known, consisted of four hundred to five hundred horses and about eighty deliverymen. The riders traveled a route from the Midwest to California. The Pony Express operated for only nineteen months. In that time, its horse-and-rider teams traveled more than 500,000 miles and delivered 35,000 pieces of mail across the American frontier. Amazingly, even though the job was hard and dangerous, every piece of mail but one was delivered.

If that sounds impressive, consider the disciples' job. They had to spread the Word of Christ across the whole known world. There weren't many people to carry this news, and they faced danger and hatred everywhere they went. But unless those brave disciples delivered the gospel to the lost, the message couldn't get out.

Jesus calls us to preach the gospel too. But some of us think we're not strong enough or smart enough or old enough to handle this job.

Just remember that *God doesn't call those who are already qualified.* He qualifies those He calls.

Start with your family and friends. Then work your way across God's frontier. The good news is only good news if it gets there on time.

LORD, TEACH ME TO SHARE THE GOOD NEWS WITH
THOSE AROUND ME: MY FAMILY, MY NEIGHBORS,
MY FRIENDS. GIVE ME THE WORDS TO SHARE AND
THE CONFIDENCE TO SHARE THEM, AMEN.

YOUR LONGEST TRAIL RIDE

I KNOW THAT I HAVE NOT YET REACHED THAT GOAL. BUT THERE IS ONE THING I ALWAYS DO: I FORGET THE THINGS THAT ARE PAST. I TRY AS HARD AS I CAN TO REACH THE GOAL THAT IS BEFORE ME. I KEEP TRYING TO REACH THE GOAL AND GET THE PRIZE. THAT PRIZE IS MINE BECAUSE GOD CALLED ME THROUGH CHRIST TO THE LIFE ABOVE.
PHILIPPIANS 3:13–14 ICB

Without a doubt, your Christian faith will be your longest trail ride. One sure way to get prickly, painful burrs of discouragement under your saddle is to start comparing your ride to someone else's. The truth is, even the Christians you most admire still have some spiritual growing to do. They're not perfect, just as you aren't perfect—until you're in heaven.

God is changing us to look more and more like Christ. But that doesn't happen overnight. It's a lifelong process.

Don't focus on the rides of others. And don't look back at the mistakes you've made along the way. Satan loves to get believers off track with unhappiness, jealousy, and arguments. He also likes to plant evil lies like, "You'll never amount to anything. Just look at what you've done!" or "You'll never be as good a Christian as she is. Why keep trying?"

In his letter to the Philippians, Paul urged them to keep their eyes on the prize: the crown of glory awaiting them in heaven. Philippians is an inspiring and oh-so-practical book. Paul encouraged the early church (and us) not to get pulled away from God by the worries of this world, past mistakes, or the actions of others.

Plant your feet in the Bible and read it daily. Learn scriptures to defend yourself against the devil's attacks. As you replace the devil's lies with God's truth, you will grow in your faith and feel more peace and joy.

Let your Bible be your compass on the trail of life. Follow it toward the blessings God has placed ahead. Forward is heavenward.

LORD, GIVE ME THE STRENGTH TO GROW IN MY CHRISTIAN FAITH—TO PRESS ON TOWARD THE GOAL OF HEAVEN. I WANT TO WIN THE PRIZE: ETERNITY WITH YOU, AMEN.

LONGING FOR HOME

THEN JESUS TOLD HIM, "BECAUSE YOU HAVE SEEN
ME, YOU HAVE BELIEVED; BLESSED ARE THOSE WHO
HAVE NOT SEEN AND YET HAVE BELIEVED."
JOHN 20:29 NIV

One time, I bought a horse from someone who felt she didn't have time to care for him. I showered this horse with hours of affection, lush pastures, and horse friends. But he never seemed to accept my farm as his home. Eventually, I called his old owner, and she was more than happy to take him back. This horse had once found his true home, and he yearned to return to it.

Like that horse, believers are offered all kinds of things by this world—friends, fortune, fame. Yet we still yearn for something we can't see. Faith is believing in God and His promises without ever seeing Him. Because we can't actually lay eyes on God, our faith can fail at times. That's why God allows times of trouble and testing: to prove our faith is real and to sharpen and strengthen it. When we read the Bible, we learn about the importance of faith. (If you want to read about some inspiring, faithful heroes in Scripture, spend some time in Hebrews 11. Scholars call it the "Hall of Faith.")

What does "walking in faith" mean? It means knowing that when I do the wrong thing, God will forgive me. It means believing that God really knows what is best for me. And it means trusting that He has good plans for me, even when things don't make sense. To live by faith means to trust God even when our days get difficult. It's how we keep going.

When it comes to Christian faith, we must believe in Jesus to one day see Him in our heavenly home.

LORD, I LONG TO HAVE FAITH, EVEN THOUGH I CAN'T SEE YOU. PLEASE STRENGTHEN MY FAITH, AMEN.

GOSPEL TRADERS

"BE CAREFUL OF FALSE PROPHETS. THEY COME TO YOU AND LOOK GENTLE LIKE SHEEP. BUT THEY ARE REALLY DANGEROUS LIKE WOLVES. YOU WILL KNOW THESE PEOPLE BECAUSE OF THE THINGS THEY DO."
MATTHEW 7:15–16 ICB

Horse traders use half-truths to sell horses for personal gain. But these small lies can create big problems, both for the horse and the buyer. Incomplete truth still isn't truth, and it's a common trick of greedy people and the devil.

Unfortunately, there are plenty of people telling half-truths about God. These false teachers mix in enough Bible facts with their lies so that it seems they're telling the truth. Whether they are doing it for money or to gain followers, their feel-good messages of flowers and sunshine give the wrong idea about God, people, and life. These ear-ticklers proclaim a false god who wants us all to be happy, rich, and popular. Now, God *is* full of grace and love, but He also expects us to turn from our sins once we accept the gospel.

Too many people have been charmed away from God's honest truth by these lie-sellers. Then, when life gets tough, these people get confused. Challenges with school, friendships, or a loved one's health can convince lie-believers that they are full of sin, that they lack faith, or that God is punishing them. Or they decide God is not a good or real God after all.

God does not promise to make you rich and popular. He never says He will keep you healthy or out of life's storms. But He does promise to carry you through all situations.

To avoid these "gospel traders," you need to know God's truths. Study the Bible, pray for guidance from the Holy Spirit, and watch the actions of the "teachers" around you. If what they do shows they love themselves more than they love God, don't buy what they're selling.

LORD, HELP ME TO KEEP LEARNING YOUR TRUTHS SO THAT I WILL KNOW WHEN SOMEONE IS LYING ABOUT YOU. GIVE ME TEACHERS AND PASTORS I CAN TRUST, AMEN.

BRINGING OUT THE BEST IN US

DON'T COPY THE BEHAVIOR AND CUSTOMS OF THIS WORLD, BUT
LET GOD TRANSFORM YOU INTO A NEW PERSON BY CHANGING
THE WAY YOU THINK. THEN YOU WILL LEARN TO KNOW GOD'S
WILL FOR YOU, WHICH IS GOOD AND PLEASING AND PERFECT.
ROMANS 12:2 NLT

Show me your horse, and I'll tell you who you are.

These special friends are like a mirror. They show who we really are—the good, the bad, warts and all. They know when we're happy or sad, at peace or in pain. They nuzzle their way into our hearts and help us work through our hang-ups, troubles, and fears. As our horses help us see our true selves, they bring out the best in us.

If we let Him, God will bring out the best in us. He, too, understands us and knows our pain and joy. He helps us work through our hang-ups and see our true selves—warts and all. Then, if we're willing to trust Him, He shapes us and makes us into the very best we can be—the people He created us to be. This walk of faith is not an easy path. But it's so worth it.

If we're to become more like Jesus—and the best "us" we can be—we must first understand that life's challenges don't *make* us who we are. They *show* who we are. Everyone has troubles. It's what you *do* with them that really matters. If a friend betrays you, do you get even? Or do you trust God to bring true friendships into your life? If we trust in God, He will use the challenges to make our faith even stronger.

Here's a truth to plant deep in our hearts: "You will have many kinds of troubles. But when these things happen, you should be very happy. You know that these things are testing your faith. And this will give you patience. Let your patience show itself perfectly in what you do. Then you will be perfect and complete" (James 1:2–4 ICB).

Trust God to use your troubles to bring out the best in you.

LORD, HELP ME SEE PROBLEMS AS OPPORTUNITIES TO BECOME MORE LIKE JESUS. BRING OUT THE BEST IN ME, AMEN.

Smooooch!

GETTING BACK ON THE HORSE

"DON'T BE AFRAID, FOR I AM WITH YOU. DON'T BE DISCOURAGED, FOR I AM YOUR GOD. I WILL STRENGTHEN YOU AND HELP YOU. I WILL HOLD YOU UP WITH MY VICTORIOUS RIGHT HAND."
ISAIAH 41:10 NLT

Riding horses can be a dangerous activity, and I will admit that I struggle with moments of fear. They usually come just before a big trail ride. Horses are big animals, and you never can tell what is going to spook one. We've all heard the saying, "If you fall off a horse, you have to get right back on." Even for longtime riders, this can be hard to do.

The same thing happens in my everyday world too. Even though I trust my life to Jesus and read His Word every day, I still struggle with fear sometimes. The truth is, fear can freeze our faith. And it gives the devil an opportunity to steal our peace. During those moments when fear is churning in our hearts, there is only one thing we should do: talk to God. In Jesus' name, we can (and should) tell the enemy to hit the road. The devil will do his best to get us off God's path. But he will lose his hold on us when we decide God is stronger than whatever we're afraid of. I think our Christian walk could be described as "falling off a horse and getting right back on." We fall off when we give in to fear or sin. We get back on when we pray and confess our sins.

Growing a stronger faith isn't easy. But if we keep getting back in the saddle after we fall, one day we will get to ride off to a life in heaven with God.

Remember: God is bigger, so you don't have to be afraid.

LORD, SOMETIMES I'M AFRAID AND DON'T KNOW WHAT TO DO. WHEN THAT HAPPENS, REMIND ME TO TURN TO YOU. GIVE ME COURAGE AND HELP ME GET BACK IN THE SADDLE AGAIN, AMEN.

CHANGING YOUR LIFE

THE TIME WILL COME WHEN PEOPLE WILL NOT LISTEN TO THE
TRUE TEACHING. THEY WILL FIND MORE AND MORE TEACHERS
WHO ARE PLEASING TO THEM, TEACHERS WHO SAY THE THINGS
THEY WANT TO HEAR. THEY WILL STOP LISTENING TO THE TRUTH.
THEY WILL BEGIN TO FOLLOW THE TEACHING IN FALSE STORIES.
2 TIMOTHY 4:3-4 ICB

O wning a horse means that we are making a promise to that horse—
and that we are willing to make some changes in our lives, like no
more sleeping in. Nothing says unconditional love like leaving your
warm, cozy bed to feed horses when it's fifteen degrees below zero
outside. Even though some changes are tough, there are many joys and
blessings that come with owning a horse.

Some people want the love and forgiveness of Jesus Christ, but
they don't want to make any changes in their lives. We must ask ourselves whether we're on a *truth quest* or a *happiness quest*. We can always
find a person, a web page, or even a church that will lie and tell us
whatever we want to hear. Like spiritual junk food, it sounds good, but
it isn't the whole truth of the Bible.

When it comes to changing your life for a horse, you know it's hap-
pening when it becomes a habit to clean out the stall, brush and feed
your horse every day, and ride as often as you can.

When it comes to changing our spiritual lives, growing in God's
truth means doing the things that make our faith stronger: having a
daily quiet time, reading devotionals, studying the Bible, praying,
going to church, and sharing our faith. Spending time with God and

His Word every day is so important to the life of every believer. God's Word is alive and active, and it will change our lives.

Truth isn't always easy to hear. But when we let our love of Jesus change our lives, we can receive all the blessings of having a relationship with Him.

LORD, HELP ME STAY AWAY FROM SPIRITUAL JUNK FOOD.
I WANT THE SATISFYING FOOD OF YOUR TRUTH, AMEN.

KEEPING THE HERD TOGETHER

DO YOUR BEST TO LIVE IN PEACE WITH EVERYONE.
ROMANS 12:18 ICB

Horse herds work together like a community. So the herd is always a bit nervous when a new horse is introduced to the group. Occasionally, we'll get a horse that just won't get along with others. A single horse can change the whole personality of our herd, making it restless and breaking up the group.

A single person can do the same thing, making others feel unsettled and dividing group members. It's sad to believe, but there are Christians out there who think it's their job to decide how holy other people are. These folks have a hard time getting along with others. They can change the way a whole group of people works together. If you've ever been unfairly judged by someone, you probably felt hurt and angry. And that's normal.

However, the devil wants nothing more than to break up God's family of believers. He wants to divide our homes, families, friendships, and churches. He encourages hurt feelings. And he uses lies, anger, and gossip to tear us apart.

Disagreements happen in all our lives, but most conflicts could be fixed if believers would remember what Jesus said in Matthew 18:15–17. In these verses, God's Word teaches us to go to the one we're having trouble with and try to make peace. Don't blame others. Don't hold on to your anger. And don't refuse to forgive. The best way to keep a "herd" together—whether it's a church, friends, or a family—is to follow what the Bible says. Stick together, build each other up, and forgive one another.

Whatever you do, never fight with that person. Instead, keep your eyes on Jesus. Ask the Lord to show you if you really are doing something wrong and to help you work on your own mistakes. Then ask God to help you forgive the person who hurt you.

When we handle our disagreements God's way, they can turn into a chance to build stronger relationships and shine for Jesus.

LORD, DISAGREEMENTS ARE HARD. SHOW ME
HOW TO HANDLE THEM YOUR WAY, AMEN.

LET YOUR LIGHT SHINE

"In the same way, you should be a light for other
people. Live so that they will see the good things
you do and will praise your Father in heaven."
MATTHEW 5:16 NCV

Horse shows are opportunities for horse and rider to show off the fancy moves and difficult routines they've practiced for months. Riders dress in their finest clothes. Horses are brushed, washed, and oiled until they gleam. The whole event gives horses, riders, and owners a chance to shine in front of others.

We also have an opportunity to shine. As children of God, we are called to live out our faith in a world that is dark with sin. Jesus said, "Be a light for other people. Live so that they will see the good things you do and will praise your Father in heaven." People around us will form an opinion about God based on what we say and do.

Are you shining? Do you keep to yourself or try to reach out to others? Most of us are guilty of spending too much time with our smartphones, computers, and games—and not enough time with people. But if we don't reach out to others, we miss out on the people God puts in our lives.

Ask God for help to truly *see* the people around you each day. As you ride to school, pray for God to show you the needs of friends and teachers. At home, try to get to know your neighbors. ***Little kindnesses could lead to conversations and even friendships.*** As you notice needs and problems around you, offer God's hope and encouragement by listening with love and care.

Most of all, pray for courage to talk about Jesus and tell what He's done for you. If you get nervous, remember that when you chose to follow Jesus, the Holy Spirit came to live inside you. He will help you shine.

So shine on, friends!

LORD, PLEASE HELP ME SHINE MY LIGHT IN FRONT OF OTHERS. I WANT TO SHOW YOUR GLORY IN ALL I DO, AMEN.

A CASE OF CHOKE

CONTINUE PRAYING AND KEEP ALERT. AND
WHEN YOU PRAY, ALWAYS THANK GOD.
COLOSSIANS 4:2 ICB

My horse Orlando believes all food belongs to him—his food, my food, and the food of the horse next to him. Because of his attempts to get *all* the food, Orlando has hurt his leg twice and suffered a bad case of choke. *Choke* is pretty much what it sounds like: being unable to swallow after eating grain that wasn't properly chewed.

Entitlement (say en-TIE-tuhl-munt) is a popular word in our culture today. It means believing you deserve things, even if you don't. Entitlement has a way of darkening our hearts with pride. We can start to feel that the world owes us a spot on the team, an A on the paper, or the latest phone or game. Entitlement can even spill over into our relationship with God when we start treating Him as if He were a genie handing out wishes.

The truth is, God doesn't owe us anything. And if our prayers are full of selfish demands, His answer will be no. If we go to God feeling that He owes us something, or if we decide how good He is based on what He gives us, then we are in danger of spiritual choke. God owes us nothing, but He *loves* us enough to give us His grace and forgiveness every day. God gives us what we need, and that's not always what we want.

Change your attitude by giving God your gratitude instead. Then your heart will be filled with His light.

LORD, HELP ME NEVER TO THINK THAT YOU
OWE ME ANYTHING. I PRAISE YOU FOR ALL THE
MANY WAYS YOU HAVE BLESSED ME, AMEN.

CHOOSE HIM

BUT TO ALL WHO DID ACCEPT HIM AND BELIEVE IN HIM HE
GAVE THE RIGHT TO BECOME CHILDREN OF GOD. THEY DID NOT
BECOME HIS CHILDREN IN ANY HUMAN WAY—BY ANY HUMAN
PARENTS OR HUMAN DESIRE. THEY WERE BORN OF GOD.
JOHN 1:12-13 NCV

Being a horse kid comes with so many decisions! Will you compete in shows? Which ones? What events will you participate in? Will you ride with your family or will you find some horse-owning friends? Will you only brush your horse's mane, or will you braid it too?

God gave us free will, which means we make our own decisions. Without free will, we would be like robots, moving only when He made us move. Free will is both a gift and a responsibility.

We have free will when it comes to love. True love happens only when it is a choice. And we cannot freely and willingly give our hearts to God unless we have the choice of *not* loving Him.

Jesus Christ gives us this choice when He stands at the door of our hearts and knocks (Revelation 3:20). But we must open the door and ask Him to come into our lives. You open the door when you believe Jesus is God's Son and choose to follow Him. That choice makes you one of God's children.

Choose today to be His child for all eternity.

Lord, I choose You. Thank You for adopting me as a "child of God." Help me grow more and more in love with You every day, amen.

RIDING RIBBONS

THIS WORLD IS FADING AWAY, ALONG WITH EVERYTHING THAT PEOPLE CRAVE. BUT ANYONE WHO DOES WHAT PLEASES GOD WILL LIVE FOREVER.
1 JOHN 2:17 NLT

Horse shows are flat-out fun. The crowds and prizes create an energy that's hard to match. Still, you don't measure the relationship you have with your horse by the number of riding ribbons you collect. Rather, the relationship is built over time with trust, patience, and facing challenges together. We feed our horses, care for them, and stay with them through the good and the bad times. In return, they give us friendship, love, and joy.

All the "stuff" of this world—things like awards and trophies, clothes and phones—are all like show ribbons that fade over time. The things of this world don't last, but God's love for us never fades. His love is *so* strong that He was willing to send His Son into the world to give His life for us.

So it makes sense to go after those things that will last forever. Instead of spending hours and hours trying to be popular or making sure you have the latest device, spend time with God and find places to serve Him with the talents He's given you. As Jesus preached in His Sermon on the Mount, "Store your treasures in heaven, where moths and rust cannot destroy, and thieves do not break in and steal. Wherever your treasure is, there the desires of your heart will be also" (Matthew 6:20–21 NLT).

We go after what we prize. Since Jesus could come back at any moment, shouldn't *now* be the time to go after things God thinks are important? Make Jesus the treasure you chase after, and you will find Him every time.

LORD, FORGIVE ME FOR CHASING AFTER THINGS THAT WILL FADE AND TURN TO DUST. I WANT TO CHASE AFTER THE TREASURES THAT LAST FOREVER INSTEAD, AMEN.

START CLACKING

ALL OF YOU YOUNG PEOPLE SHOULD OBEY YOUR ELDERS. IN
FACT, EVERYONE SHOULD BE HUMBLE TOWARD EVERYONE
ELSE. . . . BE HUMBLE IN THE PRESENCE OF GOD'S MIGHTY
POWER, AND HE WILL HONOR YOU WHEN THE TIME COMES.
1 PETER 5:5-6 CEV

Sometimes foals and even younger horses lower their heads and clack their teeth together. This behavior shows they will submit and let older horses take the lead. By clacking, the young horses show they are willing to accept a lowly place in the herd.

For us, shoveling manure could be considered the least fun part of horse ownership. It's definitely a lowly task that keeps us humble. Yet it's a necessary way of serving our horses and keeping them healthy.

Submit. Be humble. In this day and age, some people treat these as bad words. For Christ-followers, however, both are virtues that help us become more like Him. Jesus led by serving others. And He gave us an example of being humble when He washed His disciples' feet. He knew the cross was coming. Yet He bent His knees and served.

When God asks us to submit and be humble, it doesn't mean we're worth less than others. He calls us to respect one another, to be willing to depend on someone else, and to serve others. It's not enough to be humble before God. He wants us to be humble before others too. God's perfect design is for all people to love and serve each other.

How can you serve your family, friends, and neighbors this week? Ask God for some creative ideas. Then be willing to go and do the things He shows you.

And the next time your horse creates manure, remember that your animal is keeping you humble. Come to think of it, if we all started clacking, what a wonderful world it would be.

LORD, I WANT TO FOLLOW YOUR EXAMPLE OF BEING HUMBLE. HELP ME LOVE AND SERVE OTHERS, AMEN.

A FRIEND YOU CAN TRUST

"I NO LONGER CALL YOU SERVANTS, BECAUSE A SERVANT DOES NOT KNOW HIS MASTER'S BUSINESS. INSTEAD, I HAVE CALLED YOU FRIENDS, FOR EVERYTHING THAT I LEARNED FROM MY FATHER I HAVE MADE KNOWN TO YOU."
JOHN 15:15 NIV

We riders often feel a mix of fear, uncertainty, and excitement when trying out a new horse. We fear making a wrong decision. We're uncertain about our own riding skills. And we're excited about the possibilities this horse offers.

People who don't follow Jesus can feel that same mix of fear, uncertainty, and excitement about Him. Maybe they're excited by the love and forgiveness He offers, but they're afraid of what He might ask them to change or give up. Or they are worried about their past mistakes and fearful He might not forgive them. I've even heard some people say they "tried Jesus" and it didn't work. But Jesus isn't like a new game or a new restaurant. You can't just stop in and "try" Him.

Jesus is a friend we can trust. He invites us to come to Him at any time—just as we are. He will never let us down. He listens to us, guides us, and loves us no matter what. Following Jesus as our Friend means confessing with our mouths that He is our Lord and King. It means obeying Him and turning away from our sin. Trusting Him means accepting that His death on the cross pays for our sins and makes us right with God.

Follow Jesus, and you will find the Friend who will never ever let you down.

LORD, I WANT TO KNOW YOUR PERFECT LOVE. HELP ME GROW CLOSER TO YOU IN FRIENDSHIP, AMEN.

GREENER PASTURES

GOD DOES WONDERFUL THINGS THAT
PEOPLE CANNOT UNDERSTAND.
HE DOES SO MANY MIRACLES THEY CANNOT BE COUNTED.
JOB 9:10 ICB

To horse people, springtime rain usually means mud, more mud, and *lots* more mud. But just when you think it will never stop raining, the sun comes out and your pasture fills with green grass. Your horses kick up their heels, full of energy as temperatures warm and days get longer.

Just like the spring mud, our lives are messy and, at times, boring. You get up each day, go to the same school, have the same fights with your sibling. If your life feels like you're just spinning in mud, take a moment to think about how creative God is. We get so used to seeing His creation that we forget what a miracle it is!

Study the earth and how it's tilted just right in its orbit around the sun. Look around at all the different ways God shows off His handiwork in nature every day, every month, every year. God makes the sun come up and go down. He creates new snowflakes every winter and new flowers every spring. Rivers freeze and thaw; birds fly south for the winter and then migrate back as the seasons change. Animals hibernate in winter and wake up in spring. Small, cute new arrivals—foals, puppies, and rabbits—tug at our hearts.

The rain we sometimes moan about brings new life to our world. What if, instead of complaining about rain and mud, *we opened our eyes to miracles, big and small*? Fill your heart with His joy and

His promises for greener pastures. It will change the way you see everything.

LORD, HELP ME SEE—AND PRAISE YOU FOR—YOUR MIRACLES EVERY DAY. HELP ME ENJOY LIFE, AMEN.

PUT ON YOUR HELMET

PUT ON SALVATION AS YOUR HELMET, AND TAKE THE
SWORD OF THE SPIRIT, WHICH IS THE WORD OF GOD.
EPHESIANS 6:17 NLT

A big argument in the horse-riding community is whether to ride with a helmet or not. There are many reasons why you should wear a helmet, and there are plenty of reasons why some riders don't. But just as other athletes protect their heads against danger, horse riders need protection for their heads too.

As children of God, we also need protection against danger. That's why the Lord gives us strong armor to keep us safe from the devil's attacks. And part of the armor God has given us is His Word. When we put on the helmet of salvation—which means choosing to follow and obey Jesus—we are putting on protection the devil can't get through.

Make no mistake, the devil is after our minds. Sometimes our thoughts can trick us. Lies swirl through our brains: *You are worthless. You are not good enough. You will never do anything important.* When thoughts like these attack our minds, we need to remind ourselves of this truth: Jesus loves us so much that He died for us. The lies Satan hurls at us are no match for Jesus' sacrifice and His precious promises of love.

Guard and protect yourself from the devil's lies and tricks by putting on your helmet of salvation. Go ahead and say it out loud: *I follow Jesus!* Then pick up your Bible. It's your weapon of truth against the devil's lies, and it's waiting to be used. So take control and defend your-self by opening its pages. Put God's promises to work in your mind.

LORD, THANK YOU FOR PROTECTING ME FROM SATAN. HELP ME PUT ON MY ARMOR AND PICK UP THE SWORD OF YOUR WORD EVERY DAY, AMEN.

GROWING IN TRUST

THE LORD WILL KEEP HIS PROMISES. WITH LOVE
HE TAKES CARE OF ALL HE HAS MADE.
PSALM 145:13 ICB

The key to any relationship is trust. And trust is particularly important when it comes to horses. We have all had that moment when we want a horse to trust us, but the horse isn't quite sure. In those moments, we can begin to imagine how God must feel when we don't trust Him.

God faithfully keeps every one of His promises. And He never changes the way He loves us. But some people still don't believe they can trust Him. Maybe they feel He hasn't answered their prayers. Or they've had some problems they think God should have saved them from. Or maybe someone gave them a wrong idea of who God is—that He is angry or out to get them. Whatever the reasons, the Bible tells us again and again that God is completely trustworthy. He is faithful. The Bible shows us a picture of a loving, patient, and radically forgiving God who will stop at nothing to have a relationship with the people He created.

The truth is, you cannot trust someone you don't know. So getting to know God is the key to learning how to trust Him. Also, as we walk through each day with Him, we learn He wants only what's best for us. If He doesn't answer our prayers on our schedule or says no to a prayer, He has a reason.

If you are having trouble trusting God and His goodness, tell Him so. He already knows how you feel, so don't be afraid to talk honestly with Him. Treat Him like the friend He is, and He will show Himself to you.

LORD, I CONFESS I SOMETIMES HAVE TROUBLE TRUSTING YOU. GIVE ME THE COURAGE TO BE HONEST. AS I OPEN UP MY HEART TO YOU, SHOW ME WHO YOU REALLY ARE, AMEN.

HE SEEKS THE LOST

"THERE IS MORE JOY IN HEAVEN OVER ONE SINNER WHO
CHANGES HIS HEART AND LIFE, THAN OVER NINETY-
NINE GOOD PEOPLE WHO DON'T NEED TO CHANGE."
LUKE 15:7 NCV

Shopping for a new horse is always an adventure. But as exciting as it is, the best advice I have ever received on horse buying is this: be patient when looking for a horse, and the right one will find you.

In other religions, people believe they have to find their god themselves. But in Christianity, God seeks people. In fact, Jesus came to seek the lost. He once told a story about a shepherd with one hundred sheep who had one lamb go missing. The shepherd was so upset that he left the ninety-nine sheep in the field to go out and search for his one lost sheep. When the shepherd found the animal, he put it on his shoulders and carried it home. Then the shepherd called his friends and neighbors and threw a party to celebrate the return of the wandering lamb.

We are the lost lamb in the story, and Jesus is the shepherd. Think about just how important we are to God. It's hard to understand—or even imagine.

Our heavenly Father is patient with us. He doesn't want anyone to be lost (2 Peter 3:9). That's why He goes searching after those who don't yet believe in Him—just like a shepherd searching for his lost animal. And when even one lost soul is found and chooses to follow Him, all of heaven throws a party!

The next time you wonder how important you are to God, think about the story of the lost sheep. You are incredibly valuable to the Creator of the universe. Let Him find you.

LORD, I'M SO GRATEFUL YOU ARE PATIENT
AND LOVING. THANK YOU FOR NEVER
GIVING UP ON FINDING ME, AMEN.

HORSE PEOPLE

NOW WE TELL YOU WHAT WE HAVE SEEN AND HEARD
BECAUSE WE WANT YOU TO HAVE FELLOWSHIP WITH
US. THE FELLOWSHIP WE SHARE TOGETHER IS WITH
GOD THE FATHER AND HIS SON, JESUS CHRIST.
1 JOHN 1:3 ICB

Horse people are a kind all their own. Not only do I value the friendships I have with my horses, but I'm also grateful for my friendships with the horse people around me. When life "bucks" us off, it's nice to have someone there to pick us up off the ground. My horse buddies are the ones hitching up their trailers and ready to do whatever is needed for me and my ponies.

When our horses are sick, we are there for one another with wraps, medicines, or anything else that could be needed. Horse people also help each other coax horses into trailers. And we welcome one another's animals when big catastrophes like barn fires or hurricanes strike.

It's natural to want to be around people who love, help, and encourage us. As Christians, *we need to "hitch up our trailers" with others who love God*. Hanging out with other believers, helping and encouraging them to follow Jesus, and just plain loving them is called *fellowship*. The company we keep is so important when we're trying to stay on the right path with God.

Some people don't want to join a church family or a Bible study group. Maybe they're afraid they won't fit in, or they're worried about what people will think. No church is perfect. That's because churches

144   UNBRIDLED FAITH

are made up of people who aren't perfect. But God created us to need one another.

If you've asked Jesus Christ into your life as your Savior and Lord, you are a member of God's family. So let's hitch up our trailers and travel together on God's path.

LORD, THANK YOU FOR THE FRIENDSHIP AND FELLOWSHIP
I HAVE WITH OTHERS WHO LOVE YOU, AMEN.

DON'T PUT GOD IN A BOX

WITH GOD'S POWER WORKING IN US, GOD CAN DO MUCH, MUCH MORE THAN ANYTHING WE CAN ASK OR IMAGINE.
EPHESIANS 3:20 NCV

Shetland ponies have long, thick manes and tails and an extra-thick winter coat. Because of the unique way God made them, they can live in all types of harsh weather. And they would *always* rather be outside. I know this, but sometimes I can't help putting my ponies in a stall during storms. By not trusting God's design, I am putting my ponies in a box.

We can do a similar thing with God when we forget how powerful He is. We try to squish our great big God into a box when we forget He can do way more than we ask. Sometimes we are so focused on the goodness of God that we forget He is also mighty. He wants to do so much in our lives—so much more than we can think or imagine.

Over the years, God has been described in many ways: holy, caring, full of mercy and grace, loving, faithful to keep His promises, and forgiving, to name a few. Yet as pastor Charles Stanley pointed out in his book *A Gift of Love*, there is one essential thing about God that everyone can celebrate: He is *giving*. He gave us life, He gave us Jesus, and He wants to give us heaven.[3]

God's ever-giving heart allows us to go right to Him. It's incredible, but our voices matter in heaven. God *wants* to give us good gifts!

And don't forget that He *can*—because He is mighty. Don't put God in a box. Instead, remember that we serve a mighty and giving God.

THE ONE TRUE THING

I DECIDED THAT WHILE I WAS WITH YOU I
WOULD FORGET ABOUT EVERYTHING EXCEPT JESUS
CHRIST AND HIS DEATH ON THE CROSS.
1 CORINTHIANS 2:2 NCV

Sometimes when we get around horse people, we find ourselves surrounded by all kinds of know-it-alls. And in some cases, these people actually do know a lot. But these horse experts can make us feel like we don't know anything at all. That's when we need to remind ourselves of what is most important: we love our horses, and our horses trust us.

What's more, it can be so tempting to compare ourselves to other riders. *But we will never succeed at being ourselves if we are trying to be someone else.*

Our journey as a Christian should be our own too. When we are tempted to compare ourselves with other Christians, we should focus instead on the Lord. He is the One we are following, and He says, "Do your own work well, and then you will have something to be proud of. But don't compare yourself with others" (Galatians 6:4 CEV).

The truth is, we will meet other Christians along the trail who seem to know everything about God—they know every Bible verse, sing every song, and pray amazing prayers. And it's easy to feel like you're not as good or as smart as they are. But remember, all that matters is that *you* know the one thing that is most important: Jesus died on the cross to save you. If you know that, then you know the most important thing of all.

LORD, HELP ME NOT TO COMPARE MYSELF WITH OTHERS. HELP ME HOLD ON TO THE ONE TRUE THING: MY RELATIONSHIP WITH YOU, AMEN.

HUSH, HUSH

IF WE CONFESS OUR SINS, HE WILL FORGIVE OUR SINS,
BECAUSE WE CAN TRUST GOD TO DO WHAT IS RIGHT. HE
WILL CLEANSE US FROM ALL THE WRONGS WE HAVE DONE.
1 JOHN 1:9 NCV

Strangles happens! This infection swells a horse's nose and throat and makes it hard to breathe. Strangles can also spread to other horses. My horse Sven had Strangles, and he had to stay away from other horses for two months. Plus, nobody came to ride with me. If people hear your horse has Strangles, they avoid your barn as though you have the plague—and you kind of do.

The hardest part about having Strangles in my barn was admitting it. Some horse owners are so "hush, hush" about this disease that it spreads because they don't tell anyone their horse has it.

In the same way, we often try to cover up sin. But sin happens. And trying to hide it only makes it spread. Sin strangles our relationship with God. Often others are affected by our wrong choices too. They might even be tempted to follow our sinful example.

It's as if there's a tug-of-war going on inside us. We want to do what's right. We want to please God—but we still mess up and sin. Then, instead of coming clean and telling God, we try to hide from the only One who can forgive us.

If this describes you, guess what: you're not alone. Even one of the great heroes of the faith, the apostle Paul, said, "I don't really understand myself, for I want to do what is right, but I don't do it. Instead, I do what I hate" (Romans 7:15 NLT).

Don't get strangled by sin. Instead, talk to God and stay connected to Him. Then the only thing you'll spread will be your faith in Him.

LORD, THANK YOU FOR YOUR FORGIVENESS. THANK YOU FOR DEFEATING THE POWER OF SIN, AMEN.

CLEANING OUT THE TACK ROOM

DON'T COPY THE BEHAVIOR AND CUSTOMS OF THIS WORLD, BUT
LET GOD TRANSFORM YOU INTO A NEW PERSON BY CHANGING
THE WAY YOU THINK. THEN YOU WILL LEARN TO KNOW GOD'S
WILL FOR YOU, WHICH IS GOOD AND PLEASING AND PERFECT.
ROMANS 12:2 NLT

I always seem to have a lot more tack than I need. *Tack* is all that equipment we have for our horses. I have bridles, bits, saddles, and other stuff—probably enough for twice as many horses as I have.

Why is tack so fun to collect? And why do I collect more of it than I even have space for? If I didn't clean my tack room out once in a while, I wouldn't have any room left in the barn for my horses. But as cluttered as my tack room gets, my mind gets even more filled up.

Social media, the internet, and news about the world invades our lives. It's tempting to let all the bad stuff pile up in our minds. It can overwhelm our faith in very little time. And a steady diet of television programs, movies, and music that don't honor God can really bring down our thoughts, our feelings, and even our faith.

If we allow it to, this kind of junk food for our brains can change our thoughts to the point that we are no longer acting the way Jesus wants us to. By cleaning out our spiritual tack rooms every day, we can choose to stay focused on Christ instead. Prayer, Bible study, going to church, and worship are some of the ways to live His way.

When we keep ourselves soaked in His Word instead of in bad news and useless information, we can keep the world and its negative ways from creeping back in. Let's be "addicted" to God and the Bible instead of the things of this world. Then our lives will be so full of Him that the world won't be able to change us.

LORD, CLEAN OUT MY SPIRITUAL TACK ROOM.
HELP ME FEAST ON YOUR WORD AND NOT
THE STUFF OF THIS WORLD, AMEN.

PUNY PRAYERS

FINALLY, BE STRONG IN THE LORD AND IN HIS MIGHTY POWER.
EPHESIANS 6:10 NIV

As I talked about earlier, nothing gets my mind spinning and my heart pumping more than learning a horse has Strangles. This happened to one of my horses one time. After pulling the sick horse away from the others, I found myself praying, "When the others get sick with this illness, please let it go quickly." A week later, no other horses had gotten sick. That's when I discovered that Strangles wasn't my real problem. *My problem was praying puny prayers to a mighty God.*

As believers, we often limit ourselves by our own small prayers. God is capable of doing far beyond anything we can even imagine. So why do we pray for wimpy things like for Strangles to go away quickly instead of praying boldly for no more horses to get sick?

We get to talk directly to the One who is more powerful than anyone or anything in the world. God's power is bold, mighty, and strong. Think about the first line in the Bible: "In the beginning God created the heavens and the earth" (Genesis 1:1 NIV). Wow. This same God is alive in anyone who follows Him, and He bends down from heaven to hear our prayers.

The power of the almighty God raised Christ from the dead, and it can change our hearts. It can set us free from sinful habits, fix broken relationships, and give hope to the hopeless. And that power is available to every believer. Because Jesus came, no sinner is too sinful to rescue.

Whatever you are facing today, call on the power of heaven with your prayers. God is *mighty*!

LORD, FORGIVE ME FOR PRAYING PUNY PRAYERS.
HELP ME COME TO YOU BOLDLY, AMEN.

GET MOVING

WEAR THE FULL ARMOR OF GOD. WEAR GOD'S ARMOR SO
THAT YOU CAN FIGHT AGAINST THE DEVIL'S EVIL TRICKS.
EPHESIANS 6:11 ICB

Owners know that when their horses get sick, it's best not to let them lie down for too long. While there is no rule about how long a horse can be down before muscle damage begins, the sooner you can get them moving, the better.

We also tend to lie down when things get tough. In fact, one of Satan's tricks is to convince us that our lives would be easier if we would just lie down and quit. That's when God urges us to get up and keep moving forward, one faithful step after another. Life is hard, even if we love Jesus. And the longer we lie down and believe the tricks of the devil, the longer we aren't working for God.

Do you feel powerless to fight Satan? You're not. God has given us real and mighty weapons to protect us and defeat the devil's plans. He has given us a shield of faith we can use at any time. It works when you believe God's promises instead of Satan's lies. The next time you are tempted to lie down and quit, say out loud, "Satan, you are a liar. I believe in Jesus, and His blood washes away my sins. You have no power here!"

God has also provided us with the sword of truth—the Bible. When you feel attacked and start thinking you aren't good enough, find scriptures that tell you how much you are worth to Christ. (Try Luke 12:6–7 and Zephaniah 3:17 to start.) Say them—out loud, if possible—and believe their truths instead of the devil's lies and your roller-coaster emotions.

Before damage to your faith begins, get up and move. When it's hard to stand up, remind yourself that you are standing behind the God of the universe. His armor gives you all you need to stay safe and strong.

LORD, I WILL PUT ON YOUR ARMOR. I
WILL KEEP FIGHTING. GO BEFORE ME AND
SHOW ME THE WAY TO GO, AMEN.

GOD'S MASTERPIECE

YOU ARE THE ONE WHO PUT ME TOGETHER INSIDE
MY MOTHER'S BODY, AND I PRAISE YOU BECAUSE
OF THE WONDERFUL WAY YOU CREATED ME.
PSALM 139:13-14 CEV

If I added up all the hours I think about my horses, I'm sure it would be an embarrassing chunk of my day. I think about where we'll ride next time, how much I feed them, when I need to feed them again, and how blessed I feel to have such warm and loving animal friends. I plan our next road trip, think about the treats I'll get at the store next time I'm in town, and look through catalogs of bridles, bits, and other horse gear.

We think about the things we care about the most, so it's no surprise that God thinks about us all the time. He's like a proud Father who can't stop talking about His children. Not only does God love us, care for us, and rejoice over us with singing (Zephaniah 3:17), but He gives us His grace and love. God's love is something we could never earn or deserve on our own. Yet He gives it to us freely as a gift. Not only that, but the Psalms also tell us that we are the masterpiece of God's creation (8:5) and the apple of His eye (17:8). Just imagine—of all the incredible animals, plants, and stars God has made, *we are His favorite creation.* How amazing is that!

We don't always expect much in life. But listen to this: the God of the entire universe loves each one of us. God truly loves us more than we can ever understand. And He's not embarrassed at all by how much He thinks about us.

Thank You for making me a masterpiece. Help me never forget how valuable I am to You, amen.

PACKING YOUR SADDLEBAGS

*If you declare with your mouth, "Jesus is Lord,"
and if you believe in your heart that God raised
Jesus from death, then you will be saved.*
Romans 10:9 ICB

When it comes to trail riding, there's no promise that everything will go smoothly. So many things can go wrong. My horse could buck me off, a piece of equipment could break, or I could get lost or hurt. So just in case of trouble, my saddlebags are always heaping full of things to help me get through the what-ifs: my pocket knife, a water bottle, my cell phone, and a leather punch to fix equipment with.

There are also plenty of things that can go wrong on the trail of life. But when you accept Jesus as your Lord and believe God raised Him from the dead, you are packing your saddlebags with something you can be sure about: your salvation. The promise that you are saved from your sin is found in God's Word. We don't have to live our Christian lives wondering and worrying each day whether we are truly saved. God says we *are*—and that is enough.

In fact, part of our spiritual armor is called "the helmet of salvation" (Ephesians 6:17). When Jesus died on the cross, He saved us from our sins and gave us a place in heaven with God forever. But Jesus also gave us a way to survive the devil's attacks.

When the devil tries to tell you that you aren't really saved, remind him of his defeat when Jesus rose out of the tomb. Tell him that Jesus already beat him, and he has no business bringing up old sins. Use Scripture to send him running away from you.

God has given each of us the tools we need to travel the trails of life. It's up to us to use them.

LORD, THANK YOU FOR THE PROMISE THAT I REALLY AM SAVED. BECAUSE I'VE PUT MY TRUST IN YOU AND TURNED AWAY FROM MY SINS, I DON'T HAVE TO WORRY ANYMORE, AMEN.

RIDE STRONG

I CAN DO ALL THINGS THROUGH CHRIST,
BECAUSE HE GIVES ME STRENGTH.
PHILIPPIANS 4:13 NCV

Riding competitions have a way of highlighting our strengths but also our weaknesses. And if you are smart, you will use the information the judges give you to make your next ride even stronger. They may explain how to get your horse to walk or trot better. Or they may correct your balance or the way you sit on your horse.

In the same way, hard times show our strengths and our weaknesses. *We know God is in control, but some days it's hard to live like we know it.* The devil attacks us where we're weakest. And he likes to stack one trouble on top of another—like having a huge fight with one friend the same day you find out another friend is moving away.

When you are under attack, the Holy Spirit can help you be strong. For example, ask the Holy Spirit to show you the best way to comfort your friend who's moving, while also giving you the wisdom to make peace with your other friend.

There are also times the Spirit gives you the strength to do something you don't want to do but you know must be done—like forgiving that friend you argued with. Praying to the Holy Spirit for strength can make our rides stronger. With His help, we can come through our struggles more like Jesus than before.

Lord, I know that I can do all things through You. And right now, I need Your strength, amen.

LOVE, NOT FEAR

LOVE THE LORD YOUR GOD WITH ALL YOUR HEART AND
WITH ALL YOUR SOUL AND WITH ALL YOUR STRENGTH.
DEUTERONOMY 6:5 NIV

S ome people see horses as just stubborn beasts. They say horses can't really be our friends. These people often use fear to force a horse to do what they want. They end up breaking the horse's spirit. But ruling a horse with fear is not only cruel, it isn't necessary. Horses can easily become our partners if we show them kindness, patience, and love.

Some Christians use fear as a way to scare people into following God. But God does not want you to come to Him out of fear. *He wants you to come to Him out of love—because you want to.*

The good news is that there's no need for fear. You can't ever mess up too much for God. And it's never too late to choose to follow Him. When you put your faith and trust in Jesus, God promises to forgive you and give you the gift of life forever with Him.

Are you ready to let God be the ruler of your life? Will you become a willing partner with Him? Would you like to choose Him right *now*? The Bible doesn't give a specific prayer you must pray, so something kind of like this will work just fine. Pray it to God with all your heart:

Dear God, I know I am a sinner. I believe Jesus Christ, Your Son, died on the cross for my sins. I believe He rose from the dead to be my Lord. God, I am sorry for all my sins. And I invite Jesus into my life. Thank You, Jesus, for giving me the free gift of eternal life. I promise to try to live the way You tell me in Your Word, the Bible. In Jesus' name, I pray, amen. Welcome to the family of Christ!

LORD, THANK YOU FOR GIVING ME THE FREEDOM
TO CHOOSE YOU BECAUSE I LOVE YOU—NOT
BECAUSE I'M AFRAID OF YOU. HELP ME SERVE
AND PLEASE YOU WITH MY LIFE, AMEN.

HORSE ROOKIE

"Everyone will hate you because of me. But if you remain faithful until the end, you will be saved."
Matthew 10:22 CEV

W hen you start loving horses, life is all about horses and anything to do with horses. However, because we're rookies—new at this horse business—we worry about messing up. And we look to others to tell us what's right.

As a rookie in carriage driving, I was told by my instructor that I needed an overcheck. This piece of horse tack runs from the horse's back, over the head, and connects to the bit. It keeps your horse's head up. I did not feel right about using an overcheck with my horse Gus, but my instructor was very sure.

I called a carriage-driving store and asked about the equipment. The person who answered told me that using an overcheck was cruel. I am so thankful that person had the guts to tell me what I already knew deep down but was afraid to say. I am also thankful I found a new instructor.

Even in our relationship with God, we often look to others to tell us if we're getting it right instead of asking God. I didn't go to church as a child. So, growing up, I never knew about a God who loved me and had a plan for my life. I was quietly searching for Jesus on my own, but I was also afraid people would make fun of me or call me names for believing.

Do you want to obey Jesus, but you're afraid people will laugh at you, call you names, or stop being your friend? Don't let those fears stop you. Think about how much you love Jesus. And don't look for others to accept you. Instead, seek God's wisdom and approval, and you'll have His peace.

HIDDEN TREASURE

WE HAVE THIS TREASURE FROM GOD, BUT WE ARE LIKE
CLAY JARS THAT HOLD THE TREASURE. THIS SHOWS THAT
THE GREAT POWER IS FROM GOD, NOT FROM US.
2 CORINTHIANS 4:7 NCV

From newborn foals to older animals, each one of my horses has taught me something that's strengthened my relationship with God. Some of my horses were ones that no one else wanted. If God decided to, He certainly could have shown me what He wanted me to learn without these horses. But He chose an unlikely group of broken-down horses to teach me. I have found beautiful lessons in the faces and drooping bodies of these horses—animals many people would call worthless.

The world can make us feel worthless, but God values us. And He uses us to do His work. But first, we have to let Him. No one is too young or too small, too old or in too much trouble. The Bible is chock-full of misfits chosen by God to do His holy work: Moses stuttered. Joseph was hated by his brothers. David was a murderer. Jonah ran away when God called him to preach. Jacob was a thief and a liar. Samson had too little patience and too much pride.

God still used these broken-down people. Why? So that when they did amazing things, it would be clear that the power came from God and not them. Just look at me: I have a problem understanding what I read. So what does God ask me to do? Be a writer. What a crazy choice!

When God chooses us to do something, He makes it clear that our great power is from Him and not from ourselves. If you are making excuses to keep you from working for God, then it's time for you to remember who God is. Trust Him to do the impossible. If you are willing to serve Him, God will give you a way to do it.

LORD, I'M ONE OF THOSE MISFITS WHO WANTS TO SERVE YOU. USE ME AND GIVE ME YOUR STRENGTH, AMEN.

FARM CALLS

"HEALTHY PEOPLE DON'T NEED A DOCTOR. IT IS THE SICK WHO NEED A DOCTOR. I DID NOT COME TO INVITE GOOD PEOPLE. I CAME TO INVITE SINNERS."
MARK 2:17 ICB

Sometimes during emergencies it's impossible to get a horse into the vet clinic. But a *farm call* will bring the vet clinic to your barn. When we're afraid for our horses, we feel such a huge comfort when we hear the veterinarian say, "I am on my way!"

Jesus went to people's houses too. He was often looked down on because of the people He hung out with. The Jewish leaders once asked Jesus why He ate with thieves and sinners. Jesus simply said He had not come for the good people but for the sinners. His example encourages us to rub elbows with the people who need Him the most.

We build our churches and expect that hurting people will walk through the door. But the Lord tells us to go out into the world. That's often where the lonely and hurting people are.

Living our lives in a "holy huddle"—hanging out only with other Christians—makes us feel safe and comfortable. Sometimes we don't know how to act around people who think differently from us. And that can make us nervous or a little scared. So when we stick to our huddle, we don't have to deal with people who are different. But here's some amazing news: our comfort isn't tops on God's list. *Jesus calls us to spend time out of our holy huddles telling the world about Him.* All through the four Gospels (Matthew, Mark, Luke, and John), we see Jesus making His disciples *uncomfortable*. He did this by being a friend to people who were different from Him—like lepers, sick people, and sinners of all kinds.

Are you sharing God's love with those around you? What do people see when they look at your life? Do they see the humble goodness and kindness of Jesus in your face? This is a great time to start making house calls.

LORD, TEACH ME TO MAKE HEAVENLY HOUSE CALLS. I WANT TO SHARE THE GOOD NEWS WITH THOSE AROUND ME. GIVE ME A CHANCE TO TELL OTHERS ABOUT YOU, AMEN.

LOST AND FOUND

> "IN THE SAME WAY, THERE IS JOY IN THE
> PRESENCE OF THE ANGELS OF GOD WHEN ONE
> SINNER CHANGES HIS HEART AND LIFE."
> LUKE 15:10 NCV

Fly spray, buckets, and brushes are just some of the basic barn items that I'm always running out of. And I usually have to make my trip to the store right after I've returned home from a riding event. At horse competitions, these types of items seem to grow legs and wander away.

Losing something makes us worry, especially when that something is useful or valuable. When these lost objects are found, we share our good news with friends. That is how God sees us—as that lost and wandering someone who needs to be found. God rejoices over every lost sinner who repents and comes back to Him.

In Luke 15, Jesus told a story about a woman who had ten silver coins. She lost one, so she turned on the lights, got out her broom, and searched high and low until she found the lost coin. Then she called her friends and neighbors to tell them the good news.

Even though we may feel small and unimportant at times, we are loved by God. He sees us as valuable, and He searches for us until we are no longer lost. Amazingly, all of heaven rejoices for us.

The Bible reminds us to keep our thoughts on the Lord. That is the key to living a life that is marvelous, joyful, and filled with meaning and purpose. And it all starts when you begin a relationship with Jesus Christ.

You were once lost, but now you're found.

Lord, thank You that I am no longer lost. Thank
You that my life matters to You, amen.

DONKEYS VERSUS HORSES

"WHEN YOU GIVE TO SOMEONE IN NEED, DON'T DO
AS THE HYPOCRITES DO—BLOWING TRUMPETS IN THE
SYNAGOGUES AND STREETS TO CALL ATTENTION TO THEIR
ACTS OF CHARITY! I TELL YOU THE TRUTH, THEY HAVE
RECEIVED ALL THE REWARD THEY WILL EVER GET."
MATTHEW 6:2 NLT

One spring I was lucky enough to be given two donkeys. Other than having four legs and a horse-shaped face, donkeys are nothing like horses at all. In other words, they may look like a horse, but they act like a donkey. These kind, loving, and smart animals are loud when they bray. But when you pet them, they almost purr.

Both horses and donkeys like to be around other animals. But horses like to gather into packs, while donkeys will often bond with just one other donkey. Horses are also easier to scare than donkeys. And donkeys' tails and manes are stiffer and more brittle than horses' tails and manes.

Donkeys and horses look similar but are very different. In the same way, there is often quite a difference between people who *say* they follow Jesus and those who actually *do*. Just because people call themselves Christians doesn't mean they are the real thing. They may have two legs, go to church, and quote Scripture with the best of them. But that doesn't mean they follow Jesus. These phony followers don't love others or forgive them. And when they do serve God, it's so other people will see how "good" they are. These "donkeys" are not what Jesus wants His followers to be like.

The world is full of people who say they follow Jesus. But they do it so badly that people around them think loving Jesus means not loving others. How sad that, to some people, the word *Christian* has come to mean *hateful*, *two-faced*, or *phony*.

There will always be phony Christians. But it would be a terrible shame if we allowed them to be the only people who talked about Jesus.

LORD, I WANT TO BE A TRUE FOLLOWER. TAKE AWAY ANY PHONINESS FROM MY LIFE. MAKE ME INTO THE PERSON YOU WANT ME TO BE, AMEN.

RUNAWAY STAGECOACH

MAKE SURE THAT NO ONE MISSES OUT ON GOD'S
WONDERFUL KINDNESS. DON'T LET ANYONE BECOME
BITTER AND CAUSE TROUBLE FOR THE REST OF YOU.
HEBREWS 12:15 CEV

You can't sit through an entire Western movie without experiencing the spills and thrills of the stagecoach chase. The excitement in these films usually builds throughout the first half of the movie and ends with the stars trapped in a runaway stagecoach.

Consider this: holding on to your anger—even if you're right to be angry—is like being trapped on a runaway stagecoach. Anger starts when we see a situation as unfair or we feel we've been treated badly by another person. We replay the wrong over and over in our minds like a movie. And we think of all the hurtful things we'd like to say to that person. *Just like a runaway stagecoach gaining speed, our feelings of anger build and build.* But the truth is, the devil would like nothing more than to see us barrel toward a cliff and go right over the edge.

Anger is one of the devil's favorite ways to make us crash. But the choice is ours: keep blaming others or let go of our anger. Unfair and hurtful things happen in this fallen world. But when we choose to think about who we are in Christ instead of focusing on our anger, our hearts will begin to change.

Don't let anger take control of your stagecoach. Choose to let go of your feelings and praise the Lord instead. And you'll be rescued by our greatest hero, Jesus Christ.

LORD, PLEASE TAKE AWAY ANY ANGER IN MY HEART.
HEAL MY HURTS AND GIVE ME PEACE, AMEN.

YOU JUST NEVER KNOW

Answer me when I call to you, my righteous God. Give me relief from my distress; have mercy on me and hear my prayer.
PSALM 4:1 NIV

As much as we try to control our rides—the saddle, the trail, the time—most things are out of our hands. The only certain thing about horses is that you never know what they will do.

When it comes to God, you just never know what He will do either. So when He answers our prayers, it's not always in ways we expect.

Sometimes He takes us out of our comfort zones to help us see that what we thought we wanted isn't what we need. Maybe you prayed to get a spot on that team or in the play. Maybe you prayed for a certain horse to be yours. And perhaps He said no or to wait instead of yes. God doesn't always answer us the way we want or when we want. That's hard to understand, and it hurts. But remember, God sees the big picture. And, in the end, He will give us the things that are best for us. Maybe you didn't get that first horse you wanted, but now you can't imagine not owning the horse you have. God sees what we can't see.

And it's possible that God has answered a prayer, but we won't know about it until we get to heaven. We can ask God to do things our way and to fix things the way we think is best, but He is so much wiser than we are. Trust His answers.

Thanking God for the prayers He has answered in our past is a good way to remind ourselves that God always comes through—even when it's in ways we can't see or understand.

God will never stop being good, so don't stop being grateful.

LORD, I DON'T ALWAYS UNDERSTAND YOUR ANSWERS TO MY PRAYERS, BUT I KNOW YOU CARE AND ARE LISTENING. HELP ME UNDERSTAND THAT YOU ARE WORKING THINGS OUT IN THE WAY THAT'S BEST FOR ME, AMEN.

FINISH WELL

IT IS BETTER TO FINISH SOMETHING THAN TO START IT.
ECCLESIASTES 7:8 ICB

When I was young, I didn't have the chance to compete in horse shows. Then, not long ago, I was given an opportunity to enter my horse in a carriage-driving competition. This was not something I had ever considered, and quite frankly, neither had my old horse. I spent a good year getting ready for our first big day of showing. There were plenty of times I wanted to toss in the reins and give up, but I kept going. We took third place on show day—and that was out of three entries. Even though we came in last, I was happy. We had done something that some people struggle to do: we finished well.

In everything we do—whether it's something we choose to do or not—there is a finish line. Although it's nice to start well, what's more important is that we end well. That takes trusting God and His wisdom all the way to the finish line.

We don't need to win or even meet our goals, but by finishing the task without giving up, we accomplish something great. In Hebrews 12:1, the apostle Paul said, "Let us run the race that is before us and never give up" (ICB).

What job has God given you? Don't give up until He says it's finished. When we are following God, the end is even better than the beginning. It's up to us to finish well.

LORD, I WANT TO FINISH WELL. HELP ME KEEP GOING AND
NEVER GIVE UP. BLESS MY STEPS AND MY EFFORTS, AMEN.

LIGHT UP THE WORLD

JESUS WAS GETTING READY TO LEAVE IN THE BOAT. THE
MAN WHO WAS FREED FROM THE DEMONS BEGGED TO
GO WITH HIM. BUT JESUS WOULD NOT ALLOW THE MAN
TO GO. JESUS SAID, "GO HOME TO YOUR FAMILY AND
FRIENDS. TELL THEM HOW MUCH THE LORD HAS DONE
FOR YOU AND HOW HE HAS HAD MERCY ON YOU."
MARK 5:18–19 ICB

In a twinkling moment in my childhood, I decided I loved these amazing creatures called horses. Although I have not always owned one, horses have always been a part of my life. There are other horse people who fell in love with owning horses later in life, and they have a different kind of thankfulness for these beautiful animals.

As Christians, the stories of our lives can also be different. There are those who decided to follow Christ in childhood. And there are those of us who found Jesus later in life. But it doesn't matter when our stories began. What is important is that we share the stories of our faith with others.

Every fire needs a spark to get it started. And your story may be the spark that lights the fire of faith in someone's life. I have a friend who runs a horse-riding school. This school brings God's gift of horses to kids who may not be able to afford them. This is her mission field for God. It's dirty, full of flies, and filled with teenagers who bring a lot of drama with them. But by serving God this way, she has the chance to tell these kids about Jesus and the way to heaven.

Whatever your story is, the devil is standing by, ready to pour water on your flame. Don't let him put out your spark. The next time you feel as if you have nothing good to share, tell the world what Jesus has done for you. Light it up for the Lord.

Lord, help me never be afraid to share my faith. Give me the courage to tell others about You and to light up the world with Your truth, amen.

MEASURING TRUTH

FOR THE WORD OF GOD IS ALIVE AND POWERFUL.
HEBREWS 4:12 NLT

In ancient times, people didn't have devices to measure how tall their horses were. Instead, they used something that was always with them: their hands. A *hand* is still the unit of measurement for horses today. One hand equals four inches.

In today's world, many people measure the truth by what so-called experts and the internet have to say—instead of what the Bible has to say. Sadly, because of wrong information, people can end up wondering whether there really is a Creator or not. Too many people are in danger of missing heaven by only twelve inches, which is roughly the distance between our hearts and our brains. Our hearts long for a relationship with God, while our minds want to understand Him. But God is simply too big for us to completely understand.

It's true that faith plays a huge part in the life of a Christian. But so does thinking. In fact, when we look for answers to questions about God, our relationship with Him grows stronger—even if we still have questions. The internet and scientists are a great source of truth for many things. But they fall short of the Bible—the only perfect place to find answers about God. Trusting these sources over the Word of God is just like using only our hands to measure our horses: it can give us different answers about their true height.

We can count on the Bible to be true. In it, God has given us the wisdom to meet every need and every problem. Next time you feel confused, check to see what the Bible says. Ask the Holy Spirit to show

God's heart to you. Ask parents and Bible teachers to help you. God's Word is truth. It's the only measuring stick that really matters.

LORD, I WANT TO MEASURE TRUTH BY WHAT THE BIBLE SAYS. TEACH ME, GUIDE ME, AND HELP ME GROW CLOSER TO YOU, AMEN.

STEPPED-ON TOES

DEATH'S POWER TO HURT IS SIN. THE POWER OF SIN
IS THE LAW. BUT WE THANK GOD! HE GIVES US THE
VICTORY THROUGH OUR LORD JESUS CHRIST.
1 CORINTHIANS 15:56–57 ICB

When my feet are in the wrong place, my horse lets me know. I have had my toes stepped on too many times to count. The pain always reminds me how heavy horses are!

The Bible can step on our toes too. It does this by pointing out a sin we're guilty of—usually one we'd rather not admit or give up. That's when we are reminded how heavy our sins can be. The battle for our souls is over when we ask Christ into our hearts. But sin will still chase after us. The good news is that just as God's Word points out our sins, it also reminds us that Jesus died to save us from them.

Years ago, I thought I had messed up too much. The sorrow I felt for my sins was terrible. I couldn't understand how anyone, let alone God, could love me. As I was trying to figure things out, I watched a movie about Jesus. I realized it was not too late for me when Jesus said from the cross, "Father, forgive them, for they do not know what they are doing" (Luke 23:34 NIV). He was offering me forgiveness. I just needed to reach out and take it.

Jesus gives us forgiveness—something we do not deserve—because He loves us. We just need to accept His gift and follow Him. Now I get up every day and thank Him for His gift. I know I am forgiven, and God is enough.

Has God's Word stepped on your toes? Don't get stuck feeling guilty. Tell God what you've done. Then reach out and take His forgiveness. Grab hold of the eternal life He promises. In Christ, we don't have to be tangled up by sin. We are free!

LORD, BECAUSE JESUS DIED ON THE CROSS AND ROSE FROM THE GRAVE, I DON'T HAVE TO BE AFRAID. MY SINS ARE FORGIVEN AND HEAVEN IS WAITING FOR ME. I PRAISE YOU FOR THIS AMAZING TRUTH, AMEN.

ABOUT THE AUTHOR

ara Whitney grew up on a cattle farm in northern Wisconsin. After spending a decade as a radio personality, she found herself in search of that simpler life everyone talks about. She soon discovered there is no such thing as a simple life, but instead, your best-lived life is one that includes a relationship with Jesus Christ.

Cara enjoys strong coffee, fast internet, and cautious driving. She lives with her husband and two kids on a horse farm in Nebraska. Between trips to the grocery store and juggling dirty laundry, Cara has been called to tell others about the amazing news of Jesus—and she especially loves using her horses to do it.